GOVERNOR JOHN BROOKS.
(See Page 30.)

Medford in the Revolution.

MILITARY HISTORY OF

MEDFORD, MASSACHUSETTS.

1765–1783.

Also List of Soldiers and Civil Officers, with Genealogical and Biographical Notes.

BY

HELEN TILDEN WILD.

Southern Historical Press, Inc.
Greenville, South Carolina

This volume was reproduced
from a personal copy located in
the Publishers private library

All rights reserved. No part of this publication may be reproduced,
stored in a retrieval system, transmitted in any form, posted
on the web in any form or by any means without the
prior written permission of the publisher.

Please direct all correspondence and book orders to:
SOUTHERN HISTORICAL PRESS, Inc.
1071 Park West Blvd.
Greenville, SC 29611

Copyright 1903 by:
  Helen T. Wild
ISBN #978-1-63914-622-2
Printed in the United States of America

MEDFORD IN THE REVOLUTION.

MILITARY HISTORY.

At the beginning of the Revolution the resolutions passed in the town meetings of Medford, Massachusetts, were not as spirited as those of many other towns of the State; but when the time came for the citizens to choose between king and colony there were only three or four who did not stand for liberty.

In 1765, Hon. Stephen Hall, the representative, received instructions from the town which included the following confession of faith.

"Beholding with anxiety the success given to these extraordinary measures by the several laws lately enacted by Parliament tending to destroy our Trade and drain us of our Money, especially this most grievous of all Acts, commonly called the Stamp Act . . . We esteem it our bounden duty to entertain profound Respect for and pay ready Obedience to all lawful authority according to our happy constitution, and do therefore express our unshaken loyalty to his present Majesty King George III. . . . We hold in great veneration the August Body of the British Parliament and are ready to yield Obedience to the laws they shall from time to time enact *agreeable to our constitution*, but considering them as men and therefore liable to misinformation and error, whenever they require such obedience from us which is incompatible with the enjoyment of our just liberties and properties we cannot but arise and remonstrate against it." Mr. Hall was instructed to vote that the losses of Governor Hutchinson on account of the Stamp Act riot, August 26, 1765, be made up to him " upon his Application to the General Asfembly in a Parliamentary way." The other persons who sustained damages were entirely ignored. When the news of the repeal of the Stamp Act was received in Medford, the town celebrated by a great bonfire on Pasture Hill.

In reply to the pamphlet sent out by the Committee of Correspondence of Boston in 1772, the committee appointed (Messrs. Willis Hall, Stephen Hall, Tertius, Deacon Isaac Warren, Joshua Simonds and Benjamin Hall) wrote that assistance would not be wanting in the use of " proper measures as shall be thought expedient to be adopted for the preservation of our Liberties, Civil and Religious, being of opinion that a steady, uniform and persevering conduct in a constitutional way is the best means under God for obtaining that end and a Redress of all our grievances."

Rather more warmth is expressed in instructions to Dr. Simon Tufts, in regard to the payment of justices by the crown. He was told to " zeelously and vigourously exert " himself to avert so formidable an evil and frustrate the " wicked machinations of our inveterate enemies," for, if a provision which rendered the justices so dependent on the crown should become a fact, " The Ax is now laid at the Root of our Liberty with a fixed intention to hew it down."

The people of Medford met in town meeting on December 7, 1773, and heard the letter from the Committee of Correspondence concerning the three tea ships in Boston harbor. A committee was appointed to draw up resolutions and to report at an adjourned meeting, December 16. While they were adopting the report, the exciting town meeting was being held in the Old South meeting house, Boston, and when Medford's letter was forwarded, the tea was floating in the bay.

Among the Sons of Liberty who took part in the Tea Party was John Fulton of Medford. He was one of the party who disguised themselves at the house of his brother-in-law, Nathaniel Bradlee, corner of Tremont and Hollis Streets. The men were assisted by Mrs. Nathaniel Bradlee and Mrs. Fulton in assuming their disguise and in removing the stains of the evening's work.

The men were saved from capture by the authorities by the coolness of the women.

The tea troubles were not settled by making a tea pot of Boston harbor. In the latter part of 1774 it began to be whispered that some of the good people of Medford were using the forbidden beverage. A committee was appointed to " enquire if any person or persons Sells or consumes any East India teas in their families and if any such found in this Town that they cause their names to be posted up in some publick place." Then the voters, not wishing to bind their neighbors to what they would not abide by, " Voted that we will not use any East India Teas in our Families till the Acts be Repealed."

In June, 1774, the Boston Port Bill became a law, and all business in Boston and vicinity was at a stand still. It put an end to the lightering business, which was Medford's chief source of revenue.

Farmers from the east and north brought their products to Medford, which with bricks, leather and rum manufactured in the town, were transported down the Mystic river by boats or "lighters."

November 14, 1774, suffering but inflexible, the town voted, " This Town does not approve of any bricks being carried to Boston till the committees of the neighboring towns shall consent to it."

In the spring of 1775, when Boston had received money and provisions, Medford petitioned for a share of the supplies in the following words: —

" Previous to the shutting up of the Port of Boston, a great part of the Inhabitants of Medford subsisted by Brick making, and numbers of other poor Inhabitants there were employed in transporting these Bricks to Boston, where was our Market for them both in supplying the Town, and also Vessels in the Harbour, from whence they were exported to foreign Parts in great Quantities. But since by the Operation of the Port Acts, this our Trade is at an End, and those poor People are put out of Business and themselves and Families are involved in the same Calamity and distress for want of employ as are the poor of

Boston and Charlestown . . . The Inhabitants of Medford in Town Meeting assembled the 14th Instant [Mar. 14, 1775] upon Consideration of the Premises have directed us to acquaint you with our distressed Circumstances and to petition for your kind Assistance. We do therefore in behalf of said Town, pray that you would consider our unhappy Condition, and that you would (if the Circumstances of your Poor admit,) in your known Benevolence and Humanity grant us (who are suffering in the common Cause) some small Portion of that Liberality which Providence has put into your hands."

It was voted by the Selectmen of Boston to refer this to the annual meeting of the Town of Boston in May, but great events changed the current of affairs before that time, and Medford never received her " small Portion."

When General Gage began fortifications on Boston Neck, the people thought it high time to prepare to defend themselves. The Committees of Safety began to collect ammunition. Powder manufacturing was encouraged by the Provincial Congress. Stephen Hall, 3d, the representative from Medford, was one of a committee to encourage the manufacture of saltpetre. The local Committee of Safety kept a sharp watch over the powder belonging to the town, which was stored in the " Powder House" at Quarry Hill just south of Medford line. Rumor said that Gage intended to seize the powder stored there. August 27, Thomas Patten was sent to remove the town's supply to a safer place. Three days later Gage sent the troops out from Boston and carried all the ammunition remaining there, the property of several towns which had not heeded the alarm, to Castle William.

From this time forth Medford was thoroughly imbued with the spirit of resistance. November 14, 1774, it was voted to pay no more province taxes to Hon. Harrison Gray, but to order the collector to hold the same till further notice. January 9, 1775, it was voted to pay this money to Henry Gardner, Esq., Treasurer under the Provincial Congress.

The town records make mention of a Committee of Correspondence for the first time, March 13, 1775, but the Selectmen's

Order Book under date of October 2, 1774, records "Paid Moses Billings* [tavern keeper] for entertaining the Committee of Correspondence, 40s.

The Committee of Correspondence for 1775 consisted of Benjamin Hall, Esq., Ebenezer Brooks, Jr., Thomas Patten, Stephen Hall, 3d, James Wyman, Deacon Isaac Warren and Deacon Samuel Kidder.

Benjamin Hall was a member of the last General Court held in Boston, May 31, 1774, and was one of the ninety representatives who on October 5, in spite of Gage's orders, met in Salem, and behind locked doors formed the first Provincial Congress, and adjourned to Concord. Mr. Hall was put upon the committee to provide ammunition and stores. In November, seven pieces of cannon were bought and "Mr. Gill and Mr. Benj. Hall were desired to get them out of Boston to some place in the country in such manner as they may think most prudent." These were very likely stored in Medford, for on April 28, 1775, it was ordered that the "Cannon now in Medford be immediately brought to this town [Cambridge] under direction of Captain Foster."

In March, 1775, the ledger of Benjamin Hall shows that he sent to Concord a large consignment of pork, fifty axes and helves, wheelbarrows, and material for constructing barracks. There are also charges for carting, carpenter-work, and the item, "Paid James Tufts for going to Charlestown twice for gunsmith's tools."

Medford's company of Minute Men was commanded by Capt. Isaac Hall, a brother of the representative. The lieutenant was Caleb Brooks, a half-brother of Dr. John Brooks who was afterward Governor of Massachusetts. The ensign was the oldest son of Stephen Hall, Tertius.

There is hardly a name on the roll which had not been known in Medford for years. There were nine in the company named Tufts — a family resident in the town long before 1700. The names Bradshaw, Francis, Blanchard, Oakes and Pritchard dated back to the time of Governor Cradock.

* Moses Billings came to Medford, October 8, 1770; died in Medford, June 29, 1795.

As the April days advanced the people became more and more restless, and rumors were rife. On April fourteenth the Committee of Safety prevailed upon Hancock and Adams to leave Boston, and almost immediately came certain intelligence that the troops were to march into the country.

When Paul Revere " crossed the bridge into Medford town," stopped at the door of Capt. Isaac Hall, and passed on, alarming the sleeping farmers on the road to Menotomy, the people of Medford were not slow in responding. Naturally, some Medford man carried the message to Malden and perhaps farther, but his name is lost. Morning found the town almost destitute of men. Fifty-nine men had marched away in the company, and volunteers followed. Henry Putnam, who had earned the title of lieutenant in the Louisburg campaign, although exempt on account of his age, could not remain at home when there was fighting to be done, and grasping his musket, went out to give his life for freedom at Menotomy. He was one of eighty-six Putnams who were on the Lexington Alarm Rolls.

Rev. Edward Brooks went on horseback to Concord, and was in the skirmish at the bridge. Lieut. Edward Thornton Gould, of his Majesty's own Regiment of Foot, was wounded there. His life was saved by Mr. Brooks, who brought him a prisoner to Medford. In his sworn testimony Lieut. Gould said, " I . . . am now treated with the greatest humanity and taken all possible care of by the provincials at Medford." He remained in Medford until February, 1776, when he was transferred to the barracks at Concord.

Mrs. Brooks, who through the day of the battle had served chocolate to the minute-men as they passed her house, which stood in sight of the gleaming bayonets of the red coats as they passed through Menotomy, gave her self-forgetful care to her wounded enemy.

Capt. Hall and his company marched to Lexington and there joined Capt. John Brooks and his Reading company.

Capt. Brooks had left Medford only two years previous to practice medicine in Reading, and many of the men in the Medford company had been drilled by him in boyhood days, he having early developed a taste for military affairs. The combined companies overtook the British at "Merriam's Corner" and followed them to Charlestown Ferry, continuing their fire until the last of the troops had embarked. One of the Medford company, William Polly, was mortally wounded, but was brought to his home, where he died April 25.

All day the town was astir with drum and fife as company after company marched through toward Concord. When night fell, companies which arrived too late to participate in the fight were quartered in Medford, and remained there until their five days' service was over. The Medford company proceeded at once to Cambridge.

Over the roads which many had been used to travel with their ox-teams on peaceful errands, the men of New Hampshire hurried to Medford, which was designated as their rendezvous. The field officers were quartered at the "Admiral Vernon."

April 26 they held a meeting and advised the men to enlist in the service of Massachusetts Colony. They also recommended Col. John Stark to take charge of them till the Provincial Congress of New Hampshire should act. They were not well supplied with tents or ammunition. Col. Poor's regiment remained quartered in Medford for lack of the former.

In the middle of May the Committee of Safety voted that "All New Hampshire troops now in Medford if enlisted into the Colonial service under Stark and Sargent, and properly equipped, shall be provided with barracks (those who cannot be or who do not choose to enlist be provisioned home)."

A second company of militia was formed in Medford, and offered its services to the Committee of Safety. The men were ordered to hold themselves in readiness to march at a minute's notice, remaining in Medford until further orders. Cannon were planted on Bunker Hill to prevent the British going to Medford by water.

Great care was exercised that nothing of use to the British should be left within their reach. June 9, Capt. Benjamin Hall reported that a parcel of spars were on the south side of Mystic Bridge. He was directed to remove them to a place of safety.

Fire boats were constructed and kept in a place of safety, ready to be used against any vessels of the enemy which should try to come up the river.

In May, the selectmen of Medford, Malden, Chelsea and Lynn were instructed by the Committee of Safety to remove all cattle from Noddle's, Snake and Hog Islands and from that part of Chelsea near the coast. For this purpose they drew as many men as they needed from the regiments quartered in Medford.

We have a record of but two men in Medford who left the town rather than join the patriots. One was Col. Isaac Royall, the other, Joseph Thompson, a brick maker. The latter's property was treated rather roughly at first, but it was taken charge of by the Committee of Safety, who leased it to well known men of the town. The stock of bricks and lumber was seized for the use of the army.

Col. Royall went to Boston in his chariot on the Sunday preceding the Battle of Lexington, and unfortunately for him, he went armed. The testimony of his neighbors to that effect was damaging, when the question of confiscating his estates came up. He had been a member of the Council from 1752 until 1774. He was elected mandamus councillor in 1774, but never took the oath on account of public sentiment. He was one of the selectmen of Medford for sixteen years, and was moderator of the town meeting which made resolutions against the Stamp Act. The people of Medford were his friends, and were doubtless much astonished when he absented himself. Dr. Simon Tufts was his attorney, and had charge of the estates until 1778, when they were confiscated. By an agreement with the local Committee of Safety, Dr. Tufts made no remittances to the Colonel. It had been Royall's intention to retire to his West Indian estates, but the beginning of hostilities prevented his agent from engaging his passage. He constantly wrote to his friends asking their influence to procure permission for his return, and as he never was proscribed, he might have come back if he had lived until the close of the war. He died in England of small pox, a disease of which he had always had an almost morbid dread.

His grand-daughter, Elizabeth Royall Hutton, wife of Rev. Henry Hutton, and daughter of William Pepperell and Elizabeth Royall, received the title of the estates at last, and in 1804 sold to Robert Fletcher, Samuel Dexter and Fitch Hall the Royall property in Medford and Foxborough.

To protect the property of Col. Royall, Gen. Stark was invited to make the mansion house his headquarters. His wife came from New Hampshire and made her home there while the siege lasted.

On June 2, Col. Reed was ordered to collect his regiment, part of which was in Medford, and proceed to Charlestown Neck. Col. Dearborn arrived in Medford on the sixteenth and marched to Charlestown the next morning.

On the morning of the seventeenth, Stark's regiment was ordered to cross Charlestown Neck to reinforce Prescott. Under a galling fire from the British ships he marched his men across in military order.

Daniel Reed and Robert Bushby of Medford were in this detachment. They afterward served three years in the Continental army.

The Medford company was in the battle of Bunker Hill, although probably only during the latter part of the fight. Col. Henry Gardner's regiment, to which the company belonged, was at Cambridge, stationed in the road leading to Lechmere Point. Late in the day it was ordered to Charlestown. On arriving at the real Bunker Hill, General Putnam ordered part of the regiment to assist in throwing up entrenchments there. Part was ordered to the redoubt, and another detachment went to the rail fence where the New Hampshire men were stationed. Doubtless many volunteers from Medford went with Stark's regiment. We have record of a few.

Major John Brooks was at the redoubt during the early part of the day, and about 10 o'clock he was sent to Cambridge for re-enforcements and provisions. As he could find no horse, he was forced to walk to headquarters. Gen. Ward did not grant his request in time to make the re-enforcements of service. During the afternoon Major McClary of Epsom, N. H., was sent back to Medford for bandages. He crossed the dangerous Charlestown Neck in safety on the outward trip, but, returning, he was killed. His horse found his way back to the Royall House stables, and his retreating comrades found the body of the major where he fell. He was buried with honors of war in the little military burying place which long ago was obliterated. In 1849, the bodies were removed to the Salem Street Cemetery, near the Brooks' monument.

Medford was in sight of the battle and the glare of burning Charlestown. Uncertainty as to the fate of their own men made the watchers intensely anxious, but when the wounded New Hampshire men at evening were brought into town, the women had plenty to do. The field hospital was established on the main road, just south of the bridge, and the women helped the surgeons. One, Mrs. John Fulton, did a little surgical work on her own account, extracting a bullet from the cheek of one unfortunate. Many of these strangers had cause to thank the women of Medford for care when wounded or sick during the months that followed.

After the battle, the Americans began to throw up entrenchments on Winter Hill. Haste was imperative, as everyone expected the British to follow up their dearly bought victory. The provincials had few tools, having lost a large part of their scanty store at Charlestown. The General Court sent a message requesting Medford " to immediately supply Major Hale [Stark's Regiment] with as many spades and shovels as they can spare, as it is of importance to the safety of this colony that the works begun on Winter Hill be finished, and that they will be retarded unless soon supplied with tools of that kind."

When Gen. Washington took command of the army it was concluded to station one thousand militia men in and about Medford. We find record that several companies from Maine served in the town under Col. Nixon and Col. Loammi Baldwin.

These men were kept busy by constant alarms. Firing was kept up by the British ships until September 10. As the cold weather came on, the need of wood in both armies made the guardianship of the "Charlestown Wood Lots" (Middlesex

Fells) very important. The British under cover of their ships were likely at any time to cross the Mystic to get wood themselves or to intercept any intended for the Continental Army. The militia in the vicinity had the pleasure of taking some prisoners and sending them to "Washington's Headquarters at Royall's." Thomas Brooks, Esq., supplied the troops on Winter Hill with wood from his own farm. The white pines which his Majesty had reserved for his royal navy were cut down by the Continentals and used in their camps for firewood.

Powder was so valuable that all shooting for sport was forbidden, and game used for food had to be snared.

From the time Whigs were ordered out of Boston until some time after the evacuation of the town, Medford was one of the havens for the homeless people of Charlestown and Boston. Among those from the former place, we find the names Boylston, Codman, Rand, Stearns, Tufts, Kidder, Wier, Bradshaw, Swan, Cary, Edes, Harris, Stimpson and Manser; and from Boston, Hancock, Scott, Hall, Henley, Cooper, Fulton, White and Ash.

After the burning of Charlestown many very poor people came to Medford who were provided for temporarily by the overseers of the poor, and as soon as possible sent to their kinsfolk in other towns. Gen. Gage purposely sent out people infected with small pox. Precautions were taken against the dreaded disease and it was kept in check, but the next year a terrible epidemic occurred. Dr. Osgood wrote in his diary, July 9, 1776, "a melancholy day on account of small pox."

Owing to insufficient food and housing the summer of 1775 was very sickly, and was especially fatal to the little ones. Out of fifty-six deaths recorded, twenty-three were of children.

In December, 1775, a man appeared in Medford who, while he professed friendliness to their cause, was looked upon with distrust by the citizens. He lodged at Porter's Tavern, and from there wrote a letter to Washington asking for an interview at his camp. His name was Major Robert Rogers, a half-pay officer in the English army. Gen. Sullivan, then commanding at Winter Hill, was ordered by Washington to call upon the major. In reply to a question asking why he came to the camps, he replied that he wanted Gen. Washington's license to travel unmolested; as his career during the French War was far from irreproachable, Sullivan mistrusted him, and he was not allowed to come nearer to Washington than Medford. Sullivan's doubts were verified, for Rogers had been a prisoner, and was at that time on parole. A few months afterward he organized a band of Tories called the Queen's Rangers and became a colonel in the British army. If he had received entrance to the camp of Washington it would have been for the purpose of selling to the British any information he might have gained.

If spies were sent by the British, there were friends of the colonists in the town of Boston with whom Washington had communication.

Mrs. John Fulton, who has been mentioned twice before in these pages, voluntarily assumed the risk of carrying despatches into the town. She went at night on foot to Charlestown, borrowed a boat, rowed to Boston, delivered her message and returned in safety.

In September, 1775, several Medford men enlisted for the campaign against Quebec under Arnold. On September 13 the expedition started from Cambridge and camped for the night in Medford. Tradition says some of the men slept in the meeting house. They proceeded the next morning to Newburyport where they embarked for the Kennebec. Joshua Reed and Richard Cole reached home in January and February, 1776, but Samuel Ingalls of Stoneham, who was a member of the Medford company, did not return until the following October, having been taken prisoner.

The return of Capt. Isaac Hall's company, October 6, 1775, then in command of Lieut. Caleb Brooks, stationed at Prospect Hill, reported forty-one men; of these Joseph Bond was discharged in June, 1775, and Richard Pain died in August. Twenty-one of the fifty-nine minute-men are included in this roll. They enlisted for eight months directly after the battle of Lexington. Each man received his bounty coat or its equivalent. The widow of Richard Pain received money in lieu of the coat due him.

At least fifteen Medford men served under Capt. Stephen Dana at the lines before Boston. In March, Capt. Isaac Hall, in command of his company, was ordered to Dorchester Heights and served four days.

The British evacuated Boston March 17, 1776, but a few ships remained in the harbor until June. In May the Medford militia worked at Noddle's Island, building fortifications, and the next month the militia of all the towns on the coast succeeded in sending these lingerers after their companions.

As soon as the British had evacuated Boston, Washington began to send his men to New York. Bond's regiment marched the day the siege ended. Major Brooks, Sergt. Thomas Pritchard, Daniel Reed and several other Medford men were in the regiments ordered out of Massachusetts.

On June 13, 1776, when the militia had gone down the harbor for their last effort to dislodge the invaders, the Town of Medford, in town meeting assembled, voted unanimously, that " Should the Hon? Continental Congress for the Safety of the United Colonies in America declare them Independent of the Kingdom of Great Britain, the Inhabitants of said Town will solemnly Engage with their Lives and Fortunes to Support them in the Measure."

The Declaration of Independence appears in the Town Records directly following the report of the meeting at which the foregoing vote was passed, but it was not received by the town until September. On the first Sunday following its receipt, Mr. Osgood, the minister, read it from the pulpit.

On what was in the years to come to be known as Independence Day, the voters were assembled to raise extra bounty to be paid to thirty men called for " to goe to Canada." With the fate of their friends who had been imprisoned there fresh in their minds, it is not strange that many hesitated to enlist. The town offered £240 for bounty additional to that offered by the Province. As the town did not have money at hand, and must raise the amount later by taxation, Benjamin Hall and his brother Richard together advanced half of the amount, and Stephen Hall, Tertius, the remainder.

Moses and Samuel Tufts were chosen recruiting officers, and went out into "Hampshire Government or elsewhere" to enlist the men. They were empowered to pay each man two dollars on enlistment. They recruited eighteen men, and twelve men from Medford completed the quota. They enlisted for five months.

Beside the bounty already offered, seventy-four citizens added £226, 15s., 4d. to the fund for the soldiers, in sums varying from £24, loaned by Simon Tufts, Esq., "for Col. Royall," to £1. These small loans were to be paid back to those who advanced them "when they paid their next tax bills."

Before this detachment was ready the army had retreated from Canada, and these men were sent to Ticonderoga. Small pox and camp distemper ravaged the army there, and the regiments were rendered unfit for service. Many lost their lives, but eleven of the twelve Medford men lived to come home. Timothy Hall died in camp. Their hardships must have been intense, for at the next March meeting the town voted to pay them £6 per man extra allowance.

After the misfortunes at Long Island, alarm men were sent to New York. Medford was called upon to send thirteen men. A bounty was offered of £4 per man. Private subscription increased the amount to £10, 6s., 8d. No muster roll of this levy has been found. The militia called out at this time served two months. During this campaign Col. John Brooks distinguished himself at White Plains and received acknowledgments from Gen. Washington.

In the fall of 1776, drafts came thick and fast. Every fifth man in the colony was obliged to serve as a soldier or send a substitute. November 26, "The town met to draw men to go to New York" [Dr. Osgood's diary]. These men marched under Gen. Lincoln.

The winter closed in gloomily. Three days after this last draft Forts Washington and Lee were evacuated. The men at Ticonderoga were suffering privation and sickness, and there were serious fears of the return of the British to Boston. Men were constantly on duty there guarding stores and for the defense of the town. Capt. Caleb Brooks was in command of a company in Col. Dike's regiment.

At various times during the war, stores were collected in Medford at the warehouses of Benjamin Hall, and by him sent down the river to Boston. Powder in large quantities, fire arms, beef and other supplies were "boated" to the Castle and to Boston. Mr. Hall charges the Honorable Board of War at one time, "To repacking 500 bbls. of beef and setting 1200 hoops." Another item, dated 1780, is "To storing 16 tons of Cannon Balls, 18 months."

In December the islands in the bay were fortified more securely. Six Medford men, under Capt. Walton of Cambridge, worked at Noddle's Island. These militia men had not yet learned that every man was not his own captain, for three of them — one a minute-man of April 19 — after working four days, went home without a discharge. The rest worked twelve days.

December 3 another draft for the Continental army was held. Dr. Simon Tufts, Moses Billings, Capt. Thomas Brooks, John Bishop, Jr., Thomas Manning and Francis Burns were drawn, and each paid £10 for a substitute. Nearly all of these were prominent in civil affairs. Lieut. Stephen Hall, 4th, at this time went to Fairfield, Connecticut, under Capt. Benjamin Blaney, of Malden.

The men who had loaned money for bounty paid to the men who went to Ticonderoga and New York in the summer and fall of 1776, began to ask for payment in January, 1777, and the accounts were still worrying the town treasurer in the following September. This money had not been paid to the soldiers through the treasurer, but through the recruiting officers, and he was constantly harassed by unlooked for claims. To obviate this it was voted by the town that "When any future draft may be called for to March out of this State the Commission Officers be desired to consult with the Selectmen what Method is best to be taken and to procure the Men at the Expense of ye town."

Stephen Hall, Esq., Rev. Ebenezer Turell, the old minister, Lieut. Stephen Hall and others loaned money freely in this time of stress. Benjamin and Richard Hall repeated their loans time and again with a poor prospect of ever receiving principal or interest. The Hall brothers and several other residents of Medford loaned money to the federal government for military purposes.

At the close of 1776 everything seemed against the patriots. The army had been driven from Canada and the town of New York. The soldiers were in rags, and it was almost impossible to induce the militia to enlist. With Washington's army at Morristown were a few Medford men who had enlisted for the war. The militia were with Gen. Lincoln at Peekskill.

Washington's victories at Trenton and Princeton revived the courage of the colonists. Messengers carried the news far and wide. January 4, Medford "had news of the success of our army at Jersey" [Dr. Osgood]. Washington immediately sent out some of his most trusted officers, among them Col. John Brooks and Capt. Thomas Pritchard of Medford, to inspire enlistments in the sixteen battalions of infantry and other branches of the service which he had authority to organize. In January, Francis Tufts and Jonathan Farley enlisted for the war. In February William Burditt and Richard Creese entered the artillery. At the March meeting bounty was voted to encourage enlistments. Joses and William Bucknam enlisted on the day of the meeting, Daniel Bayley the next day, and others followed, until Medford had over forty men in the Continental army for three years or the war.

All through the spring and summer men and women were busy in their several ways for the support of the army. The women and children carded and spun, knit and sewed the much-needed clothing for the soldiers; the men attended to their stock of guns and ammunition. Lieut. Stephen Hall, 4th, and Lieut. Jonathan Porter drilled the men who had taken the places of the thirty-seven men which their militia company had sent to Gen. Washington. Midsummer brought the bad news of the capture of Fort Ticonderoga and the battle of Hubbardton, Vermont, where Col. Ebenezer Francis was killed. He was a native of Medford and lived there until 1766, when he went to Beverly. He organized a regiment and marched to Ticonderoga in January, 1777. His chaplain said of him, "No officer was so noticed for his military accomplishments and regular life as he."

When Burgoyne's army had been captured and were in convention in Massachusetts, a party of British officers on parole were strolling through West Medford and stopped at a farmhouse where they found the mother of the colonel. In answer to her questions they told her that they had seen his dead body, and one of them produced the colonel's watch and gave it to her. His private papers were restored later.

In August, 1777, Col. John Brooks and his whole regiment volunteered to go to the relief of Fort Stanwix, and Thatcher in his "Military Journal" gives the credit of the success of the expedition to the wit of the colonel, who suggested that a messenger with bullet-riddled clothing should be sent to the British camp to report the coming of a force of Americans as numerous " as the leaves of the trees."

On the twenty-fifth of September news of the first day's battle at Saratoga came to Medford. It had been fought on the seventeenth. Nearly every man who was in service from the town was in Gates' army. Lieut. Col. Brooks' regiment was in the thick of the fight. During the evening it kept Breyman's riflemen at bay. October 7, Burgoyne was obliged to fight or retreat. When the battle was at its height, Brooks again distinguished himself. He has been called the "Hero of Stillwater." His regiment was ordered to take a redoubt occupied by Breyman. He commanded Capt. Bancroft of Reading, Massachusetts, to lead the charge. He knew personally almost every man in the captain's company; they were old friends and neighbors of Medford and Reading. Not hesitating an instant, Bancroft waved the sword and cried, "Come on, boys, and enter that fort!" Then, leading his men, went over the parapet. Surprised at the suddenness of the assault, the enemy wavered, and the whole regiment rushed into the fort. The Medford men who made that charge were William Cutter, Francis Tufts, Aaron Tufts, George Tufts, Daniel Bailey, John LeBosquet, Henry LeBosquet, and John LeBosquet, Jr.

Just here a Medford tradition must be modified. Brooks' History of Medford says that Sergt. Francis Tufts was promoted to adjutant on the field at White Plains. This cannot be true, for at that time he was at Ticonderoga. On October 7, 1777, he was promoted to ensign, so we can save the story, but change the scene.

Francis Tufts at Stillwater, seeing the standard bearer fall, caught up the flag, and holding it high in air, bore it at the head of the regiment, over the redoubt. He was commissioned ensign that day by Gen. Gates. Afterward he received several promotions, and was made adjutant in 1780.

The day after the battle, Gen. Gates determined to attack Burgoyne, and sent Gen. Nixon against what he supposed to be a detachment of the enemy, but which proved to be the main army. He was warned at the last moment, and the regiment was saved from certain defeat. More than half of the Medford men were in Nixon's brigade.

Burgoyne's surrender brought English troops to Medford, this time as captives. Hessians were quartered at Winter Hill, and officers on parole lodged at Porter's Tavern, in the market place. These men were very respectfully treated by the inhabitants. Dr. Osgood frequently received the Hessian chaplain. Benjamin Hall entertained him at dinner, and English officers were frequent guests at tea drinkings and parties.

Capt. Caleb Brooks was stationed at this time in Cambridge, guarding the English troops there. Capt. Blaney of Malden served there three months, and in his company were several Medford men. Each of them was paid one dollar by the town for each day's service. There were apprehensions at this time that the British would come from New York to rescue their prisoners.

The Medford men in the Northern Army, except those under Col. Greaton, who remained at Albany, went into winter quarters at Valley Forge, December 19, 1777.

Capt. Bancroft wrote to a kinsman at this time, "I hope, sir, if my family should stand in need of your assistance you will be ready to afford it. It has been out of my power to do anything for them, even so much as to send home any money . . . I was obliged to give half a dollar for one pint of bread and milk . . . We have some hard trials to meet yet." All are familiar with the dreadful privations of the army before the winter was over.

Rev. Edward Brooks, the volunteer at "Concord Fight," obtained an appointment as chaplain of the frigate "Hancock," in 1777. The vessel was captured the next month, and her crew were made prisoners at Halifax. The officers were placed on parole.

Mr. Brooks' wife sent him money by Capt. Salter, one of the Tory prisoners of war who were to be exchanged for American prisoners at Halifax.

When the ship returned it brought a letter from Mr. Brooks, pleading for the exchange of himself and his room-mates, thirteen in number. He was "exchanged for Parson Lewis," and left Halifax for Boston, January 29, 1778. During his imprisonment he contracted small pox, from the effects of which he never recovered. He was not able afterward to do active service for his country, but helped financially by contributing bounty money.

As the records quaintly express it, "agreeable to the resolve of April 20th 1778," Medford was called upon to furnish a quota for the army. Seven men, members of Capt. Brooks' company, enlisted for nine months and arrived at the rendezvous at Fishkill, June 21, 1778. These men belonged to a levy raised for the defense of the northern frontier, from which troops had been withdrawn for the campaign in the neighborhood of Philadelphia. At the same time three men enlisted for eight months and went to North River, New York. A few days after another detachment went to Rhode Island. This was the third quota sent there, eleven men having served there during the spring and summer of 1777. These men who enlisted in July, 1778, were to join the five thousand men under Sullivan, who, with the coöperation of the French fleet, hoped to drive the British from the state. Owing to a great storm which damaged the fleet and ruined the tents and powder of the militia, the expedition proved a failure.

In the summer of 1779 six men were sent to Fishkill, having enlisted for six months. These men received in the vicinity of thirteen hundred dollars bounty (Continental money). The New England troops, including militia, composed the left wing of the army and were stationed at West Point and its vicinity.

In October, eight men enlisted for three months, and were ordered to Clavarack, or Cloverick, as it was spelled in Medford. The French fleet again failing the provincials, Washington was prevented from carrying out his plan of reducing New York, and the three months' men not being needed, were discharged before their term expired.

Accounts in those days are very puzzling to our understanding, as they were made out in lawful money, depreciated money, Spanish dollars and in gold. Barrett Rand, who went to Fishkill with the six men mentioned above, showed his good judgment by taking part of his bounty in corn (six bushels at fifty dollars), which was more stable property than Continental dollars. The scale of depreciation was constantly changing, but a few comparisons can illustrate the changed conditions.

October 2, 1774, Capt. Moses Billings entertained the Committee of Correspondence and charged forty shillings. February, 1781, Mr. Thomas Bradshaw charged £193, 10s. for entertaining the recruiting committee.

In 1780, Capt. Ebenezer Hall was paid £270 for eighteen pairs of stockings; the same amount was charged for nine years' rent of the "Garrison House" in hard money.

About this time Elizabeth Francis (Ma'am Betty, who kept the Dame School,) received five shillings for a pair of stockings, showing that five shillings in silver was worth fifteen pounds in depreciated money.

The term of service of the Massachusetts men who enlisted during the early part of 1777 expired at the close of 1779. Efforts were made to induce them to re-enlist, but the majority refused. Their families were suffering at home, they had endured bloodshed and famine, and they had lost faith in the promises of Congress.

The condition of John Symmes of Medford illustrates the

financial condition of all. He came home ragged and emaciated. He received his pay in currency, with which he bought a yoke of oxen. He sold them later, receiving the same kind of money, which he hoarded a little too long; for meanwhile its value had changed and he paid it all for a bag of Indian meal.

In 1780 Medford sent sixteen six months' men into the field. They were provided with clothing and equipments by the town. Under the inspiration of the celebration of July fourth, thirteen men enlisted. Striplings and veterans who had seen service in New York made up this quota. They came home six months later with nothing but discharge papers in their pockets, which became passports to the hearts of the people, who kindly lodged and fed the footsore travellers. The amount due the men according to the sworn statement of the selectmen was £148, 8s. 8d. hard money. In February they had not received a penny of it. When it did arrive, it was in worthless bills.

As these men returned in penury, there came another call for fourteen men for three years.

Already the little town of less than a thousand inhabitants had furnished over two hundred men to serve their country—many of them enlisting more than once. The town had sent her sturdiest sons; some of them were even then in Washington's army. Where could fourteen men be found? The selectmen and recruiting officers were assisted in their efforts to raise men and money by Jonathan Patten, Col. Richard Cary (formerly of Charlestown, but during the war the tenant of the Royall House), and Ebenezer Hall, Jr. A month passed; no money and no men were forthcoming. The quota was at last filled in May. One of these recruits was Josiah Cutter, boatman, forty-seven years old. His name appears on the Lexington Alarm Roll. Six were negroes. These men were probably not all residents of the town. Some of the negroes bore Medford names, and may have been sent as substitutes by their masters.

In 1781 about a dozen men credited to Medford enlisted for the war. In 1782, three men, perhaps more, were recruited, but the levy of 1780 was the last large one made on the town during the war.

When names are found which were not common in the town, the men were probably apprentices in the tanneries, brick yards, coopers' shops, etc. Some of Medford's young men enlisted from other towns for similar reasons. Nathaniel Polly who was at work in Framingham enlisted for that town, and Jonas Dickson who was learning the ship carpenter's trade in Chelsea enlisted there.

Essex County surnames may be accounted for by the presence in the town of sailors who were attached to vessels on Mystic River. The merchants and manufacturers of Medford owned quite a large fleet of sloops which plied between the town and the West Indies, and along the Atlantic coast. When the war interrupted trade it is probable that these vessels became privateers, although we have as yet found no positive record.

Benjamin Hall was interested in the galley "Willing Maid" (carrying four guns) sailing from Salem, 1782, Capt. John Savage, master. In 1781 it is recorded that a "shallop" was fitted out by John Bishop and Willis Hall and commanded by Capt. Nailer Hatch "of Medford," to carry a cargo to Connecticut to be exchanged for flour or grain for the Medford market. Capt. Hatch was not taxed in Medford; his home was in Malden. He had served his country as captain of a militia company and as second lieutenant of a privateer. In 1783 he commanded the armed brig "Lady Washington." With such a man in command, the little Medford vessel did not run away from any craft of the enemy which by any chance could be taken by her guns.

October 19, 1781, Cornwallis surrendered. The news was brought to Newport by Captain Lovett on Wednesday, the twenty-fourth, he having left Chesapeake Bay the day after the surrender. The news came to Medford Friday. Dr. Osgood wrote in his diary that night, "It is not Doubted by ye Generalty but I wish to have it from authority."

The next evening he wrote, "News of yesterday confirmed by authority." In all probability, Richard Creese was the only Medford resident who could have been at the surrender of Yorktown. He was in Knox's artillery.

The general rejoicing in the town was somewhat saddened by the news of the death at Yorktown of Col. Alexander Scammel, who had been stationed in Medford during the siege of Boston, and had been looking forward to the close of the war, when he could come to "that Mystical place," as he called it, to claim his bride.

When peace was declared the people welcomed back the battle-scarred veterans, who took their old places on the farms, in the shops, and on the river. Here and there a place was vacant, but private sorrow was lost in the universal joy that peace had come and the country was free.

Dr. Osgood's sermon, preached when the war cloud of 1812 overhung the country, voiced what every patriot had felt. "I have not forgotten, nor can I ever forget while consciousness abides with me, my own mental suffering during the period of our former war. Through eight long years, whose lingering pace, while hope was deferred and the heart sickened with pain and anguish, seemed without end, a burden lay upon my spirits by day and by night almost too heavy for frail mortal to sustain. . . . Thus, daily lamenting and praying against the miseries of the war, I passed through that most gloomy portion of my past life from 1775 till the transporting sound of peace in 1783."

Soldiers and Sailors Credited to Medford.

In compiling the following list of soldiers, I have used no names which are not distinctly credited to Medford in Town or State Archives or, in a few cases, Records of Pension or War Department.

Medford men served in Col. Cyprian How's Regiment in Rhode Island, 1780. In Col. Ephraim Wheelock's Regiment at Ticonderoga, 1776, were eighteen "Hampshire Government men," who were part of Medford's quota, whose names are unknown.

Gerrish's and Baldwin's Regiments at Sewall's Point, Chelsea, Winter Hill and on Mystic River, 1775, contained Medford men.

In Blaney's Co., Thatcher's Regiment, February to April, 1776, to serve before Boston, there was a large proportion of Medford militia.

The roster of Capt. Hall's Co. which served at Dorchester Heights is badly mutilated. It contains the following surnames, —Greenleaf (Corp.), Tufts, Jr. (Corp.), Robbins, Watson, ——l Tufts, Jr., Hendley, Tissick, Tufts (four men), Blanchard, Jr., Lawrence, Putnam, Butterfield, Teall, ——l Harris, Floyd, Blanchard, Dowse, ——ster, Francis (two men), Symonds (two men), Smith, Winship. These are not noted in the following list, but most of them can be identified as members of the militia in service at Lexington, or at other places in the vicinity of Boston, during the siege.

Where no reference is given, service is recorded in Archives of State of Massachusetts. Volume and page refer to "Massachusetts Soldiers and Sailors, War of Revolution," published under direction of the Secretary of the Commonwealth. Space here will not permit the details which can be obtained from these sources.

It was my first intention to include vital statistics, etc., given in records of the City of Medford only, but I have gathered information in some cases from family histories, pension papers, probate records, histories of adjoining towns, and letters from descendants of the men recorded.

I am indebted to Dr. E. C. Booth, historian of the Tufts family, Mr. W. F. Bucknam, historian of the Bucknam family and others, of Stoneham, Mr. B. D. Corey, historian of the City of Malden, and Mr. A. G. Loring of Woburn for assistance in identifying many not recorded in Medford.

ALBREE, JOHN. Dana's Co., McIntosh's Regt., March, 1776; Capt. Caleb Brooks' Co., Dike's Regt., Dec. 1776, 3 mos. service; vol. 1, p. 103. Paid money for bounty to men enlisting for Canada, July, 1776; assisted in building hay fence at Bunker Hill. Born Nov. 9, 1757; son of Joseph and Judith (Reeves); cousin of Gov. John Brooks of Mass.; lived near Rural avenue, Medford; married, Jan. 6, 1793, Lydia, daughter of William and Rebecca Tufts; went to Acworth, N. H., soon after marriage; removed to Salem, Mass.; occupation, general trader and tallow chandler; died in Salem, Nov. 6, 1842; buried in Albree tomb, Howard Street Cemetery, Salem.

ANTHONY, JONATHAN (Anthoney, Antony). At Sewall's Point, 1775, and in R. I. 2 mos., 8 days, 1777; vol. 1, pp. 277 and 280. Joined Canadian Expedition, July, 1776. (Town records.)

ANTHONY, JONATHAN, JR. At Cambridge and Sewall's Point, 1775; in N. Y. 9 mos., 1778-79; age 25 in 1778; vol. 1, p. 279. Born Jan. 21, 1753; son of Jonathan and Catherine (George); married Lois Wey of Lexington, March 6, 1777; taxed in Medford 1773 to 1778 inclusive. [I think Jonathan and Jonathan, Jr., refer to the same man. Jonathan, Sr., died in Woburn, 1807, aged 86.] Free negro.

ANTHONY, WILLIAM. Enlisted for 3 yrs., 1777; deserted Jan. 13, 1778; vol. 1, p. 280. Born Sept. 14, 1759; son of Jonathan and Catherine. Negro.

BAILEY, DANIEL (Bayley). Enlisted for 3 yrs. or the war, June, 1777; Bancroft's Co., Jackson's Regt.; transferred to Invalid Corps Sept. 1, 1779; discharged March, 1780; vol. 1, p. 449; loaned money for bounty paid to men enlisting for N. Y., Sept., 1776; received money for "2 mos. deficiency in the army," Oct. 29, 1779. Taxed in Medford, 1776. One Daniel Bayley married Elizabeth Mullet of Cambridge, March 28, 1776.

BAMFORD, THOMAS. Served at Noddle's Island, Dec., 1776; vol. 1, p. 557.

BEDIN, JACOB. See Bredin.

BERNARD, JOHN. Child's Co., Greaton's Regt.; reported deserted; vol. 1, p. 986.

BINFORD, THOMAS. Loaned money for bounty paid to men enlisting for N. Y., Sept., 1776; received bounty for joining Continental Army at Cloverick (Clavarack) for 3 mos. (selectmen's order book, Oct., 1779). Brickmaker; taxed in Medford, 1760 to 1796; married Ruth Tufts, May 18, 1767; died Dec. 16, 1796, aged 58; buried in Salem Street Cemetery, Medford.

BINFORD, WILLIAM. Private, Lexington alarm; served at Prospect Hill, 1775-76; vol. 2, p. 55. Born April 3, 1755; son of William and Phebe Manser, who were married Jan. 10, 1754. In 1775, Thomas Binford was taxed two polls for self and William Binford. Thomas Binford was chosen guardian by William, a minor, 18 yrs. of age, April 8, 1773.

BLANCHARD, AARON. Served at Boston, 1776, also guarding stores at Boston, Dec., 1776, to Feb., 1777; paid money for bounty to recruits enlisting for Canada July, 1776; residence given Cambridge Precinct and Medford; vol. 2, p. 141. See Aaron, Jr.

BLANCHARD, AARON, JR. Private, Lexington alarm; paid money to persons enlisting to go to N. Y.; vol. 2, p. 142. Son of Aaron (periwig maker) and Tabitha (Floyd); born Sept. 2, 1751; taxed in Medford, 1776, '77, '78.

BLANCHARD, ANDREW. Private, Lexington alarm; at Prospect Hill, 1775-76, and at Boston, 1776-77; loaned money for bounty paid to recruits for army in N. Y., Sept., 1776; vol. 2, p. 143. Son of Aaron and Tabitha (Floyd); born July 21, 1754; taxed in Medford, 1775.

BLANCHARD, HEZEKIAH. Loaned money paid to recruits going to Canada and N. Y., 1776; received gun and blanket money, Nov., 1776; served guarding stores Dec., 1776, to March, 1777; vol. 2, p. 145. Born in Malden, Jan. 4, 1728; son of Samuel and Sarah (Pratt); married, 1st, Susanna Dexter, Feb. 22, 1754; 2d, Sarah Hall, Oct. 6, 1763; occupation, tavern keeper; died Aug. 24, 1803; buried in Salem Street Cemetery, Medford. His tavern stood on Main street, between South street and Cradock bridge.

BLANCHARD, HEZEKIAH, JR. Received bounty for joining army at Cloverick (Clavarack), 1779 (selectmen's order book). Enlisted for Canadian Expedition, July, 1776; went to Ticonderoga. (Petition for extra bounty, town records, vol. 3). Born Sept. 3, 1758; son of Hezekiah and Susanna (Dexter); married, 1st, Elizabeth Tufts, Dec. 16, 1784, and 2d, Eunice Floyd, Jan. 1, 1797; spent part of his married life in Milton, Boston, and Charlestown; succeeded his father as tavern keeper; died Mar. 17, 1818; buried in Tomb 15, Salem Street Cemetery.

BLANCHARD, JOHN. Enlisted Nov., 1776, for 3 yrs.; reported deserted June 1, 1778, but was probably taken prisoner, as he returned Mar. 20, 1779, and was in service, 1782; age in 1781, 22 yrs.; vol. 2, p. 148. Received payment for bounty due him, April 22, 1791. (Town records.) Son of Aaron, Jr., and Tabitha (Floyd); married Rebecca Tufts, who died 1821, aged 62; died Dec. 13, 1798, aged 38; buried in Salem Street Cemetery.

BLANCHARD, SAMUEL, JR. At Prospect Hill, 1775 and 1776; lieutenant in Capt. Blaney's Co., 1778; vol. 2, p. 154. Son of Samuel, Jr., and Sarah (Cutter); born in Malden, June 23, 1749; baptized in Medford, June 25; married Martha Smith of Woburn, Jan. 11, 1776; taxed in Medford, 1770, '78, '79, '80.

BLANCHARD, SYLVANUS. Loaned money to pay bounty to recruits for army in Canada and N. Y., 1776; served guarding troops of convention, 1778; vol. 2, p. 155. Taxed in Medford, 1777 to 1792; occupation, brickmaker; son of Samuel and Sarah (Pratt); born April 11, 1738; married Sarah Grover of Malden, Nov. 28, 1764; died in Malden, Aug. 5, 1800.

BLODGETT, NATHAN. Loaned money for bounty paid to recruits for army in N. Y., Sept. 1776; served at Noddle's Island, 1776; reported deserted (went home without discharge); vol. 2, p. 197. Born Sept. 10, 1737; son of Nathan and Abigail (Converse); married Mary Whitmore, Apr. 27, 1775; taxed in Medford, 1777; non-resident member of Cambridge N. W. Precinct Baptist Society, 1787; resident of Cambridge at time of marriage.

BOND, JOSEPH. At Prospect Hill, 1775; discharged June 7, 1775; vol. 2, p. 259. Born May 22, 1749; son of Daniel and Elizabeth Barnard (born Bemis); married Anna Lawrence May 10, 1769 (Bond's Genealogies); died Dec. 30, 1775; came to Medford from Watertown, May 12, 1773.

BOYD, JOHN. Enlisted for 3 yrs. for Malden, 1777; residence, Medford; vol. 2, p. 359. One John Boyd came to Medford, 1765, age 4 yrs., in care of Wm. Faulkner.

BOYLESTONE, THOMAS. Served at lines at Boston, 1776; vol. 2, p. 371. Son of Richard and Mary (Abrahams); baptized April 3, 1760; occupation, brazier, in Charlestown; married Oct. 27, 1808, widow Mary (Hay) Farnsworth; his family resided in Medford during the Revolution. (Wyman's Charlestown Families.)

BRADSHAW, ANDREW. Private, Lexington alarm; loaned money for bounty paid to recruits for army in N. Y., 1776; drafted to join Walton's Co. at Cambridge and to go to Noddle's Island; went home without discharge; vol. 2, p. 422. Born Feb. 26, 1753; son of Stephen and Mary; taxed in Medford, 1775.

BRADSHAW, THOMAS. Private, Lexington alarm; loaned money for bounty paid to recruits for army in N. Y., 1776; vol. 2, p. 423. Born July 8, 1743; son of Stephen and Mary; married Martha Tufts, Nov. 26, 1772; died Sept. 1, 1802; received a pension; occupation, tavern keeper; proprietor of the " Fountain House," Salem street, Medford; buried in Salem Street Cemetery.

BREDIN, JACOB. (See Bedin, vol. 1, p. 883.) Served at Prospect Hill, 1775; vol. 2, p. 456. Came to Medford from Malden, with wife and two children, Nov. 24, 1770; taxed in Medford, 1771, '72, '73, '74; probably son of Samuel and Sarah, born Jan. 26, 1738-9, in Malden.

BROOKS, CALEB. Lieutenant, Lexington Alarm; in command of Medford company, Oct., 1775; commissioned captain, June, 1776; in Col. Dike's Regt. at Dorchester, Aug. and Sept., 1776, for defence of Boston; guarding stores at Boston, Dec. 1776 to March, 1777; guarding troops of convention at Cambridge, 1778; vol. 2, p. 570. According to letters of Col. Alexander Scammel, Capt. Brooks must have been at Ticonderoga, 1778. Baptized Oct. 30, 1737, son of Caleb and Mary (Wyer); married Jan. 1, 1767, Mary Kidder, daughter of Samuel; died Feb. 4, 1812; buried in Tomb No. 19, Salem Street Cemetery; half brother of Gov. John Brooks; occupation, brickmaker.

BROOKS, REV. EDWARD.* Volunteer at battle of Concord Bridge, April 19, 1775; brought home a wounded English officer, a prisoner, and took care of him until recovery; chaplain of frigate "Hancock;" a prisoner at Halifax, 1777-78. (See —— Brooks, vol. 2, p. 567). Born Nov. 4, 1733; son of Samuel and Mary (Boutwell); graduated at Harvard, 1757; married Abigail Brown, daughter of Rev. John and Joanna (Cotton) Brown of Haverhill; died, 1781; buried in Oak Grove Cemetery, Medford.

BROOKS, JOHN. Major, Lexington alarm; served until the disbandment of the army, 1783; vol. 2, p. 576. Made sub-inspector of the army by

*His brother Samuel was one of Committee of Correspondence, Exeter, N. H.

Washington, March 24, 1778, to act under Baron Steuben (autograph letter in Medford Public Library); at the battle of Saratoga, he, the lieutenant-colonel, was in command of Col. Jackson's Regt.; a personal friend of Washington, who entrusted him with several important missions; president of the Order of the Cincinnati in Mass., succeeding Gen. Lincoln; governor of Mass., 1816 to 1823; there was never a dissenting vote to his election cast in his own town. Born in Charlestown (later, Medford, and now Symmes Corner, Winchester); son of Caleb and Ruth (Albree); baptized in Medford, May 31, 1752, (church records); studied medicine with Simon Tufts of Medford; began practice in Reading, Mass.; succeeded Dr. Tufts in Medford at the close of the war; married Lucy Smith of Reading, 1774; died in Medford, March 1, 1825; buried in a tomb in Salem Street Cemetery; monument erected to his memory in centre of the burying ground. For more extended account, see Histories of Medford and Reading.

BROOKS, THOMAS, 3D. At Prospect Hill, 1775-76; vol. 2, p. 587. Taxed in Medford, 1776-77; born June 5, 1756; son of Samuel and Abigail (Hastings); married Parnel Boylstone, 1786; settled in Charlestown; called 3d in Medford because two older men of the same name resided in the town.

BROWN, GEORGE. Enlisted for 9 mos. July 9, 1778, and again, June 9, 1779, for 9 mos.; age 16; residence given Medford and Mystic; vol. 2, p. 623. Born Jan. 18, 1766; son of Ephraim and Sarah, of Stoneham.

BROWN, JACOB. Enlisted for 9 mos., 1779; residence Medford and Mystic; vol. 2, p. 629. Born in Stoneham, Jan. 31, 1749-50; son of Ephraim and Dorothy; married Ruth Knight of Stoneham, Aug. 26, 1773; resident of Stoneham, 1784.

BROWN, JAMES. Enlisted May 17, 1781, for three yrs.; age 22; occupation, mariner; vol. 2, p. 633. Son of Ephraim and Sarah, of Stoneham. (History of Stoneham.)

BRYANT, EBENEZER. Received money for enlisting to go to the Castle (selectmen's order book, Oct. 3, 1779). Son of Capt. Joseph and Elizabeth Bryant of Stoneham; born Sept. 7, 1758; yeoman; married Sarah, who afterward married James Putney; Ebenezer's will, dated June 19, 1804, was filed Aug. 11, 1804.

BUCKNAM, EBENEZER (Bucknam, Buckman). Enlisted for 6 mos., 1780; age 17; vol. 2, pp. 758 and 763. Taxed in Medford, 1783. (See James.)

BUCKNAM, JAMES. Enlisted for 6 mos., 1780; age 17; vol. 2, pp. 757 and 764. Possibly son of James and Mary (Goddard), who came from Malden, 1764. In the list of their children the names James and Ebenezer appear.

BUCKNAM, JAMES, JR. Private, Lexington alarm; vol. 2, p. 764. Probably same as James Bucknam, who served in Hall's Co., at Prospect Hill, 1775. Taxed in Medford for first time, 1777; married Margaret Sables, Feb. 12, 1778. Called Jr. because another of the same name, older than he, lived in Medford, 1775.

BUCKNAM, JOHN. Private, Lexington alarm; served under Walton at Cambridge and Noddle's Island; vol. 2, p. 759. Loaned money for bounty paid to men enlisting for Canada, July, 1776, and N. Y., Sept., 1776. Taxed first in Medford, 1769, and every year thereafter until 1779, when he resigned office of highway surveyor, as he was going out of town; taxed as non-resident until 1781, when he again appears as resident, until 1798; married Phebe Bucknam, 1776.

BUCKNAM, JOSES. Militia service, 1776-77; enlisted for 3 yrs., March 3, 1777; vol. 2, p. 764. Made prisoner Feb. 3, 1780 (Records War Dept.); confined in prisons in England and Ireland; residence given Malden, Shirley and Medford. Son of Joses and Mary (Sprague) Bucknam. He was brought up by his grandfather, Bunker Sprague; married Nabby Hay of Reading, Sept. 19, 1786; went to Mason, N. H.; his widow died in Glenburne, Me. (W. F. Bucknam.)

BUCKNAM, WILLIAM. At Prospect Hill, 1775; enlisted for 3 yrs., 1777, and for 6 mos., 1780; age (1780) 21 yrs.; made sergeant Aug. 1, 1780; vol. 2, p. 765. Born in Malden, April 30, 1759; son of James and Mary (Goddard); taxed in Medford, 1780 to 1803; died in Medford April 2, 1823. Pensioner. Pension certificate does not mention service at Prospect Hill, but records that he was in Hale's Co., Stark's N. H. Regt., from Jan. 1, 1776, to Jan. 1, 1777, beside the service for three years and a half, as above. Another, William Bucknam, went to Claremont, N. H., and the Prospect Hill service may belong to him. William Bucknam, 2d, appeared in Medford, 1803.

BURDITT, WILLIAM. Loaned money to pay bounty to men enlisting for Canada, 1776; enlisted for 3 yrs., 1777; sergeant of artillery artificers; vol. 2, p. 828. Married Mary Oakes, Feb. 2, 1784; her gravestone is in Salem Street Cemetery; he died June 13, 1788; first taxed in Medford, 1771. Jos. Burditt, Jr., of Malden, died 1749; children, Jacob, Jesse, Joseph, Nathan, Tabitha, and William. One was a posthumous child, born between Sept., 1749, and Sept., 1750. (Index, Probate Office, original paper missing, 1902.)

BURNAM, JOHN. Enlisted for 3 yrs. or the war, 1777; residence also given Malden; vol. 2, p. 887.

BUSHBY, ROBERT. Enlisted in Sargent's N. H. Regt., 1775; enlisted for 3 yrs., 1777; vol. 2, p. 933. Born Jan. 30, 1748; son of Robert and Mary.

BUTTERFIELD, ABEL. Private, Lexington alarm; served at Prospect Hill, 1775, and at Dorchester Heights, 1776, vol. 2, p. 960; also enlisted for Canadian Expedition, 1776; went to Ticonderoga; (petition for extra bounty, town records, vol. 3.) Born in Menotomy, Dec. 30, 1759; son of William and Mehitabel (Chamberlain); married Frances (Calef) Pool, widow of Richard, Jan. 5, 1783; died Oct. 23, 1793; taxed in Medford 1779 to 1793.

BUTTERFIELD, STEPHEN. Served at lines at Boston and at Noddle's Island, 1776; vol. 2, p. 965. Born in Menotomy, Dec. 30, 1759; son of William and Mehitabel (Chamberlain); taxed in Medford, 1780 and 1781.

CALLENDER, JOHN. Private, Lexington alarm; served 5 days; vol. 3, p. 30. Taxed in Medford, 1774-75. Probably son of Eleazer Callender and Sarah (Hillar) Bound of Boston; born Sept. 19, 1747; died in Alexandria, Va., Oct., 1797. Captain lieutenant, Gridley's Regt. of artillery; enlisted April 25, 1775; captain June 1, 1775. At battle of Bunker Hill, ammunition was sent him which could not be used in his guns; he retreated, was accused of cowardice and cashiered; exonerated and restored to rank by Washington. He was a prisoner at Long Island, August, 1776; exchanged; served in artillery from 1777 to 1782; vol. 4, p. 30.

CAMBEL, THOMAS. Served in R. I., 1777; vol. 3, p. 39.

CARRIL, JOHN. Enlisted for 3 yrs., May 4, 1781; age 24; vol. 3, p. 144; served for Woburn, 1777, '80; a stranger there.

CARY, WENHAM. Name given also William and Windham; enlisted, 1778, for 6 mos.; age 35; vol. 3, p. 179. Taxed in Medford, 1778 and 1779. See Windham or Wenham Carey or Carrey of Boston. Negro, age 40; vol. 3, pp. 138, 141.

CLARK, JOHN. Private, Lexington alarm; vol. 3, p. 595. Probably son of John and Mary (Smith), born June 10, 1752. The *Boston Gazette and Country Journal*, March 12, 1770, gives in a list of wounded at Boston Massacre, "a lad named John Clark, about 17 yrs. of age, whose parents live in Medford, apprentice to Capt. Samuel Howard." Clark died in Medford, May 26, 1778.

CLEFTON, JOSEPH. Private, Lexington alarm. Paid money to persons going to Canada, 1776; vol. 3, p. 617. Married Abigail Hadley, Nov. 10, 1774; living in Medford after 1800.

COLE, RICHARD. Private, Lexington alarm; in service at Prospect Hill, 1775; enlisted for Quebec, Sept. 12, 1775; vol. 3, p. 780.

CONERY, DANIEL (Conory, Conry, Connery). Private, Lexington alarm; at Prospect Hill, 1775; vol. 3, pp. 889 and 903. Came from Stoneham to Medford, May 8, 1764, with widowed mother, Sarah; taxed first in Medford, 1764.

CONERY, PETER. Private, Lexington alarm; vol. 3, p. 889. Brother of Daniel mentioned above; born in Stoneham, June 24, 1747; son of John and Sarah; taxed first in Medford, 1768; married, 1st, Mary Fowle, Oct. 13, 1774; 2d, Elizabeth Wakefield, June 9, 1777; died in Stoneham, Feb. 4, 1802. In 1764, the head of this family was Isaac, brother of Daniel and Peter. On pages 889, 907, and 908, vol. 3, there is given the service of Isaac, Daniel, and Peter (residence not stated) in companies that are known to have been made up in part from Medford. Isaac married Hannah Jackson, Feb. 5, 1766.

COOCH, ISAAC. Private, Lexington alarm; vol. 3, p. 916 (probably Cook).

COOK, ISAAC. Enlisted for 3 yrs., 1777; reënlisted for 6 mos., 1780; age 23; vol. 3, p. 925. Born, 1757; from Charlestown, 1759, with Joseph and Margery (Dickson), his parents; from Bowdoinham to the Eastward, 1766; from Charlestown, 1771; taxed in Medford, 1781 to 1787. Isaac Cook, son of Joseph Cook, late of Cambridge, laborer, age " 20 yrs. last Jan.," chose Benj. Teel of Medford to be his guardian, March 17, 1777. Feb. 14, 1816, Polly Cook, widow of Isaac, late of Charlestown, victualler, who died "within 60 days past," asked that an administrator of his estate be appointed; he died in West Cambridge and left six " infant children."

CREESE, RICHARD (Creas, Crease, Creass, Creese). Drafted to serve at Noddle's Island and Cambridge, Dec., 1776; served guarding stores at Boston, 3 mos., Dec., 1776, to Feb. 1, 1777; in Continental Army, Feb. 22, 1777, to May 15, 1779; loaned money to pay bounty to men going to Canada, 1776; vol. 4, pp. 99, 100, 103. Born in Roxbury, March 14, 1732-3; son of Richard (mariner) and Elizabeth (Tucker); married Hepsibah Cook, Dec. 4, 1755; he is buried in Eustis Street Cemetery (Roxbury), Boston, Mass.

CROWELL, AARON (Croel). Private, Lexington alarm; corporal in service at Prospect Hill, 1775; vol. 4, pp. 130 and 185. Came to Medford with his wife and family, 1751; died Feb. 24, 1795.

CUTLER, WILLIAM (See William Cutter). Enlisted, Nov., 1776, for 3 yrs. for Beverly. In service, 1780.

CUTTER, EBENEZER. Received money for joining Continental Army at Cloverick (Clavarack) for 3 mos. (selectmen's order book, Oct. 22, 1779). Occupation, blacksmith; son of Daniel and Patience (Hall); born Jan. 23, 1758, in Medford; married Mehitable Morrison, Oct. 3, 1784. He removed from Medford to Newburyport; lost his left arm in 1785 by explosion of cannon; pensioner. See other service under name Ebenezer Cutler; vol. 4, p. 321.

CUTTER, JOSIAH. Private, Lexington alarm; in service at Prospect Hill, 1775; enlisted for 3 yrs., 1780; age 47. Son of Nathaniel and Elizabeth; baptized March 7, 1734; taxed in Medford, 1765 to 1790; wife's name, "Mollie"; his bounty was paid by Rev. Edward Brooks. (Usher's History of Medford, p. 165.)

CUTTER, JOSIAH. Enlisted for 6 mos., 1780; age 16; vol. 4, p. 332. Possibly son of Josiah mentioned above, as height, complexion, etc., are alike in both descriptions, but there is no record of birth in Medford. Josiah Cutter, nephew of above and son of Nathaniel and Submit (Whitcomb) of Sudbury, was born May 7, 1763.

CUTTER, SAMUEL, of Charlestown, ensign in Capt. Hall's Co. 37th Regt. of Foot, and at Bunker Hill. Son of Samuel and Anne (Harrington); married Susanna, daughter of Ebenezer and Rachel (Tufts) Francis of Medford, 1757; killed by being thrown from a wagon, 1791; buried in Arlington.

CUTTER, WILLIAM (Cutler, Cuttler). Residence given, Medford, Beverly and Charlestown; ordered to join Paterson's Regt., Nov. 17, 1776; Francis' Regt. at Bennington, enlisted Feb. 12, 1777, for 3 yrs.; in service for Beverly, 1778; Tupper's Regt., 1780; vol. 4, pp. 335, 336, 345. Son of Samuel and Susanna (Francis), born July 15, 1759; married, 1st, Hannah Cutter, April 29, 1783; 2d, Lydia Cutter (widow), Nov. 9, 1818; died in West Cambridge (Arlington), Nov. 28, 1846; a monument erected by friends is inscribed, "A soldier of the Revolution who served during the war and was for many years a pensioner. He was in several engagements and once made a prisoner, though always distinguished for his bravery." A nephew of Col. Ebenezer Francis; taxed in Medford, 1784, '85, '86, and '88.

CUTTER, WILLIAM. Bancroft's Co., Jackson's Regt.; enlisted for 3 yrs. or the war; mustered at Boston, March 16, 1777; Wade's Co., same regiment, Jan. to March 10, 1780; enlisted March 20, 1780, in Greaton's 3d Mass. Regt.; at West Point, Jan. 25, 1781, age 21; in service, Sept. 1, 1783; vol. 4, p. 336. Son of Ebenezer and Eleanor (Floyd), born Feb. 24, 1759; married, June 21, 1789, Rebecca (born, 1765), daughter of

John Cutter of Medford and Mary (Hill); called Jr. at time of marriage; he was foreman in one of the Medford distilleries; afterward kept toll house at Cambridge bridge; died in Boston, July 27, 1800, and was laid in Granary burying ground; Rebecca, his widow, a resident of Medford, drew a pension, 1840; their daughter, Rebecca, married Isaac Sprague, a ship builder of Medford. (Cutter genealogy and pension records.) Taxed in Medford, 1784, '85, '86, '88. [The town records give date of birth as above, but other records, one year later.]

DAVIS, JONATHAN. Private, Hall's Co., Lexington alarm; at Prospect Hill, 1775, and '76; enlisted for 3 yrs., 1777; vol. 4, p. 514. Taxed in Medford, 1775. Cutter's History of Arlington says, "Jonathan Davis and Hephzibah Winship, residents — perhaps because of the military occupation and environment of Boston, 1775-76 — married, 29, Feb., 1776, in Menotomy"; also, "Jane Hinds, born 1758, married, 1st, Jonathan Davis, and 2d, Francis Locke."

DEXTER, PAUL. Private, Lexington alarm; served at Prospect Hill, 1775; drafted to serve at Noddle's Island and Cambridge, 1776; loaned money to pay bounty to men enlisting to go to N. Y., 1776; vol. 4, p. 725. Jos. Bucknam was appointed guardian, 1747, of Paul, age 6 yrs., son of Timothy Dexter, late of Leominster. Moses Bucknam became his guardian, 1757. (Probate records.) Taxed first in Medford, 1766; held various town offices; died in Medford, Dec. 31, 1808. Paul Dexter of Boston married Elizabeth Wade of Malden, March 24, 1767. (Malden records.)

DECKSON, ASA (Isaac Dickson?). Served 6 mos., 1780; vol. 4, p. 632.

DICKSON, ISAAC (Dixon). Joined Canadian Expedition, July, 1776; went as far as Ticonderoga. (Town records.) Enlisted for 6 mos., 1780; age 22; vol. 4, p. 756. Born in Medford, March 21, 1758; son of Josiah and Anna (Francis), daughter of Samuel of Medford; parents came to Medford from Charlestown, 1755; taxed in Medford, 1778.

DICKSON, JONAS. Private, Lexington alarm, Chelsea Co.; served at Cambridge, 1775; in Baldwin's Regt., April, 1776; enlisted for 3 yrs., 1777; residence, Medford and Chelsea; vol. 4, pp. 757 and 801; received a pension; baptized, Sept. 21, 1755; son of Josiah and Anna (Francis); married Elizabeth Gill, May 27, 1783; died Oct. 25, 1821; buried in Salem Street Cemetery.

DOWSE, [SAMUEL?]. Served at Dorchester Heights, March, 1776; vol. 4, p. 938.

DUNSTER, WILLIAM. Enlisted for 6 mos., 1780; vol. 5, p. 69.

EARL, WILLIAM. Seaman, Ship Alliance, under Paul Jones; enlisted at Nantes, France, Nov. 21, 1779; discharged at Boston, Sept. 6, 1780; lost one leg in battle; on list of pensioners made up from Dec. 31, 1781, to Dec. 31, 1787, age 22; vol. 5, p. 151. Taxed in Medford, 1788 to 1813; occupation, tailor; married Martha ———; had five daughters and one son born in Medford. Died in Suffolk Co., Mass., Sept. 12, 1821. (Pension records.)

EDES, POMP or POMPEY. Enlisted for 3 yrs. for town of Concord, 1777; residence given Medford and Boston; vol. 5, p. 211.

FARLEY, JONATHAN. Private, Hall's Co., Prospect Hill, 1775; transferred to artillery, April 28, 1775; served at Hull, 1776; enlisted for the war, 1777; age 28, in 1782; residence given Medford and Stoneham; vol. 5, p. 501.

FARRINGTON, WILLIAM. Fifer, Lexington alarm; enlisted for 3 yrs., 1777; reported drummer, 1780; received 200 acres of land, or $20 in money, 1801; residence, Malden, 1801; vol. 5, p. 550. Married Ruth Batts of Malden, Sept. 29, 1789; occupation, cordwainer; widow, Ruth, asks that estate be administered, April 7, 1802. Ruth married, 2d, John Oliver. (Probate records.) Also, see History of Malden (Corey), p. 814.

FISHER, JOHN. Enlisted for 9 mos., 1778; reënlisted for 9 mos., 1779; age 23; "engaged for Medford"; vol. 5, p. 701.

FLORENCE, ABRAHAM (Flourance). Enlisted, 1777, for 6 mos. in R. I.; reënlisted Dec. 18, 1777, until Jan. 1, 1778; vol. 5, p. 807. One Abraham Florence of Boston married Dorcas Sylvester, Nov. 30, 1788. (Boston records.)

FLOYD, ANDREW (Floyed). Private, Lexington alarm; served at lines in Boston, March 19 to April 5, 1776; loaned money to pay bounty to men going to Canada, July, 1776; drafted to serve at Noddle's Island and Cambridge, 1776; vol. 5, p. 812. Received bounty for joining army at Clavarack (selectmen's order book, Oct. 22, 1779.) Taxed in Medford, 1771 to 1782; married Elizabeth Bradshaw of Medford, Oct. 31, 1765; residence at that time, Roxbury; died in Cambridge Nov. 12, 1789. Probably served in R. I., 1780, in Col. Cyprian How's Regt. One of several Medford names found on this roster, vol. 5, p. 809.

FLOYD, BENJAMIN. Private, Lexington alarm; served at Prospect Hill, 1775; at Noddle's Island, Dec., 1776; loaned money to pay bounty to men enlisting for Canada and N. Y., 1776; vol. 5, pp. 810 and 812. Occupation, mason; died June 5, 1798, aged 64; buried in tomb, Salem Street Cemetery.

FLOYD, BENJAMIN. Served in R. I., 1 yr. from Jan., 1776. (Pension rolls.) Enlisted July, 1780, for 6 mos.; age 27 (archives of Mass. and records of War Department). Born in Medford, Jan. 9, 1753; son of Benjamin and Ruth; married Martha Savels, Jan. 7, 1779; died Oct. 2, 1823, aged 71; buried in Salem Street Cemetery. Martha drew a pension as his widow.

FLOYD, BENJAMIN. Served in Continental Army, Feb., 1777, to Dec. 31, 1779; reported deserted, 1780.

FRANCIS, BENJAMIN (Frances). Served at Prospect Hill, 1775; vol. 6, p. 6; also, 2 mos. in R. I., 1777; vol. 6, p. 2. How's Regt. in R. I., 1780; no residence given; (6th name, vol. 6, p. 6). Probably son of Benjamin and Lydia (Converse); born Sept. 6, 1759; died in Baltimore; uncle of Lydia Maria Child, the abolitionist.

FRANCIS, JOHN. Served at Dorchester Heights, March, 1776; loaned money to pay bounty to men enlisting to go to Canada and N. Y., 1776; vol. 6, p. 8. (See John, Jr., son of Lieut. John.)

FRANCIS, JOHN, JR. Private, Lexington alarm; vol. 6, p. 9. Son of Lieut. John and Dorothy (Coffin), born, 1736; taxed first in Medford, 1757; married Jane Teel, June 3, 1777; died, 1786. Called Jr. in 1775, because his kinsman, John (born, 1724, died April, 1776), was living in Medford.

FRANCIS, JOHN, JR. Paid money for bounty to men going to Canada and N. Y., July and Sept., 1776; vol. 6, p. 9. Probably son of John and Deborah (Carter) of Medford; born April 6, 1760.

FRANCIS, JOSEPH. Served at Prospect Hill, 1775; vol. 6, pp. 3 and 10; served 3 mos., 1781, age 39; no residence given; vol. 6, p. 3 (9th name). Born June 17, 1741; son of Joseph and Elizabeth (Harris).

FRANCIS, NATHANIEL. Served at Prospect Hill, 1775-76, and at Dorchester Heights, March, 1776; vol. 6, p. 11; also, 2 mos. in R. I., 1777; vol. 6, p. 3. Enlisted in Canadian Expedition, 1776. (Town records, vol. 3.) Taxed in Medford, 1778, '80; son of Nathaniel and Phebe (Frost), born Oct. 13, 1752. Died in Sterling, Mass., in Jan. or Feb., 1812.

FREEMAN, PRIMUS. Served 9 mos., 1778, age 36; bounty paid by Hezekiah Blanchard, Jr., vol. 6, p. 49. Taxed in Medford, 1778, '79, and '80. Free negro. Probably came from Reading; family took the name Freeman when freed from slavery. (History of Reading.) Warned out of Medford, 1784 and 1791.

FULTON, ROBERT. Drafted for service at Noddle's Island and Cambridge, 1776; enlisted for 3 yrs., 1777; in service, 1781; vol. 6, p. 201. Residence given Boston; vol. 6, p. 199. He came from Boston to Medford about 1774, when patriots began to leave the town; taxed in Medford, 1776 to 1786. Robert (of Boston) married Elizabeth Ingraham, Aug. 3, 1769.

GIBBS, JAMES. Sergeant, residence given Medford, Sudbury and Charlestown; enlisted for 3 yrs., 1777; in service, 1782; served 6 yrs.; vol. 6, p. 383. Residence, 1818, Charlestown, Mass.; born in Scotland, 1752; died Feb. 6, 1825; married Abigail Stimson of Charlestown, Feb. 4, 1777; she was pensioned as his widow.

GOWEN, JOHN. Served at lines at Boston, 1776; vol. 6, p. 694. Probably son of Hammond and Mary (Crosswell), born in Charlestown, July 31, 1760; taxed in Medford as a non-resident, 1783 to 1789.

GREEN, ISAAC. Served in Medford, 1775; residence Lexington; vol. 6, p. 806. Enlisted for 9 mos., 1778; age 23; sergeant, July 8, 1777, to Jan. 1, 1778, in R. I.; vol. 6, p. 807. Also served in N. Y. Son of Samuel Green of Lexington, Stow and Charlemont, Mass. Born in Stow, June, 1756; married Eleanor Tufts of Medford, Feb. 5, 1778; died Feb. 27, 1790; occupation, cordwainer; was an apprentice in Lexington, 1775, but resided in Medford after marriage.

GREEN, THOMAS. Served at Tiverton, R. I., May 29 to July 1, 1779; vol. 6, p. 836. Received bounty from Town of Medford.

GREENLEAF, ISAAC. Loaned money for bounty paid to men enlisting for Canada and N. Y., 1776; served at Noddle's Island, 1776; vol. 6, p. 850. Born in Medford, May 27, 1744; son of Stephen and Mary; married, 1st, Mary Tufts, Dec. 17, 1772; 2d, Sarah Rhodes, April 30, 1778; died Feb. 20, 1807.

GREENLEAF, JONATHAN. Corporal, Lexington alarm. (See company roll.) Served at Dorchester Heights, 1776; loaned money for bounty paid to men enlisting for Canada and N. Y., 1776; vol. 6, p. 850. Born June 9, 1754; son of Gardiner and Catherine; married Joanna Manning, May 5, 1778; died Aug. 13, 1801.

GRIFFIN, ROBERT. Engaged for Town of Medford, 1779; age 49; deserted at Springfield; vol. 6, p. 885. Received bounty from Medford.

GUEST, MICHAEL (Gest, Gess). Enlisted, March 16, 1781, for 3 yrs.; "engaged for Medford"; age 26; occupation, farmer; vol. 4, p. 370.

HADLEY, DAVID. Private, Lexington alarm; loaned money to pay bounty to men enlisting to go to N. Y., 1776; vol. 7, p. 16. Taxed in Medford, 1776-82; came from Stoneham, 1762; born in Stoneham, Sept. 11, 1744; son of Samuel and Abigail (Richardson); married March 16, 1769, Eunice Richardson; lived in Medford, on the east side of Spot Pond.

HADLEY, JOHN. Private, Lexington alarm; vol. 7, p. 17. Born in Stoneham, Aug. 23, 1749; son of John and Sarah (Williams).

HADLEY, MOSES. Private, Lexington alarm; loaned money to pay bounty to men going to Canada, July, 1776; vol. 7, p. 18. Taxed in Medford, 1776 to 1782; son of Samuel and Abigail (Richardson); born Aug. 22, 1756; came to Medford with parents from Stoneham, 1762; married Mary Peirce, Nov. 19, 1776; of Charlestown, 1791; bridge-keeper at Cambridge bridge.

HADLEY, SAMUEL, JR. Private, Lexington alarm; loaned money for bounty paid men going to Canada, July, 1776; vol. 7, p. 19. Came with wife Rebecca (Knight) from Stoneham to Medford, 1768; son of Samuel and Abigail (Richardson); born Oct. 13, 1732; lived next to his brother, David (see above), just south of Stoneham line, Fulton street; died 1803 or 1804; taxed in 1803, but not in 1804.

HADLEY, THOMAS. In Bond's Regt., 1776. (Pension paper.) Received money, Oct. 3, 1779, from Town of Medford for enlisting to go to the Castle, probably for service recorded vol. 7, p. 20. Born in Stoneham, July 29, 1758; son of Anthony and Abigail (Green); married Mary Nagle of Stoneham, May 8, 1778; taxed in Medford, 1780; resident of Medford, 1818.

HALL, FRANCIS. Private, Lexington alarm; at Prospect Hill, 1775-76, as sergeant; commissioned 2d Lieut., 1776; lieutenant at Winter Hill, 1778; vol. 7, p. 79. Taxed in Medford until 1811, probable date of death; married Elizabeth ———, who died 1810; son of Stephen Hall, Tertius, and Sarah (Keisar); brother of Lieut. Stephen Hall, 4th.

HALL, ISAAC. Captain of Medford company, Lexington alarm; served at Prospect Hill, April 19, 1775, to Sept. 1, 1775, and at Dorchester Heights, March, 1776; vol. 7, p. 82; was at Battle of Bunker Hill; acted as deputy commissary for Continental Army, 1775-76. Son of Andrew and Abigail (Walker); born Jan. 24, 1739; married Abigail Cutter, Oct. 8, 1761; occupation, distiller; died Nov. 24, 1789. In Aug., 1789, he disposed of all his property and left no will; his wife died Sept. 25, 1825.

HALL, MOSES. Sergeant, Lexington alarm; at Dorchester Heights, March, 1776; loaned money to pay bounty to men going to N. Y., Sept., 1776; loaned money to United States Government for war purposes. Son of Capt. John and Mary (Keisar); born 1750; married, 1st, Martha Sprague of Malden, Nov. 28, 1775; married, 2d, Hannah ———; lived in Charlestown in later years; occupation, distiller; taxed in Medford, 1771 to 1789.

HALL, PRINCE. Enlisted for 9 mos., 1778; age 30; vol. 7, p. 105. Receipt signed by himself for bounty received on enlistment can be seen at state archives. Free negro; taxed in Medford, 1778 and 1779; he was the author of a petition to the House of Representatives urging the abolition of slavery in Massachusetts. He was the founder of Free Masonry among negroes, receiving his degrees from a military lodge, consisting of British soldiers, in Boston, March 6, 1775. Married Phebe, a slave of Mrs. Lydia Bowman Baker, of Boston, who set her free. Their home was on Phillips street, Boston, where he died Dec. 7, 1807. See archives of Prince Hall Grand Lodge, F. and A. M.

HALL, PRINCE. Enlisted for 3 yrs., April 7, 1777; died Dec. 18, 1778; vol. 7, p. 105. Rev. David Osgood records in his diary, April 1, 1777, "Prince ran away last night." Mr. Osgood at that time boarded with Mr. Richard Hall, whose negro servant, Chloe, married Prince, a negro servant of Stephen Hall, Esq., Sept. 15, 1772.

HALL, STEPHEN, 4TH. Ensign, Lexington alarm; commissioned 1st Lieut., June 17, 1776; served under Capt. Blaney, Thatcher's Regt., which was ordered to Fairfield, Ct., on or before Dec. 16, 1776; company contained thirteen Medford men; loaned money for bounty paid to men going to Canada, 1776; vol. 7, p. 112. Served as recruiting officer and drill master in Medford all through the war; committee of safety, 1777; loaned money to the United States Government for military purposes. Son of Stephen Hall, Tertius, and Sarah (Keisar); born Jan. 3, 1745; married Mary Hill of Menotomy (Arlington), July 12, 1770; died in Revere, 1817.

HALL, TIMOTHY. (Also given, Timothy, Jr.) Drummer, Lexington alarm; served at Prospect Hill, 1775; died at Ticonderoga, Sept. 18, 1776; vol. 7, p. 114. Son of Timothy and Mary (Cutter); born Oct. 24, 1753.

HAMON, JOHN (Hammond?). Enlisted for Southborough, 1777, for 3 yrs.; residence Medford; vol. 7, p. 196.

HANKER, CATO (Hancock). Enlisted for 8 mos., 1778; served in New York; vol. 7, p. 228. Cato Hancock was taxed in Medford, 1777; Cato Hanker, 1779; owned real estate in Medford; veteran of French War. One Cato Hancock married, in Boston, Nancy Faddy, July 3, 1791.

HARRIS, JOHN. Enlisted for 3 yrs., 1777; in service, 1780; vol. 7, p. 345. Probably son of Josiah and Millicent (Estabrook) of Charlestown; born Jan. 31, or Feb. 5, 1752.

HARRIS, SAMUEL. Served at Dorchester Heights, 1776; enlisted for 3 yrs.; return dated Feb. 19, 1778; died in service, May 19, 1778; taxed in Medford, 1771, 1772 and 1775; he was in business as a baker in Charlestown, but lost his property by fire, June 17, 1775, and returned to Medford; married Elizabeth Hall, Nov 25, 1773; she, with her children, received state aid; the estate of Samuel Harris received bounty due him, May 2, 1785. Son of Josiah and Millicent (Estabrook); born Aug. 15, 1749; his estate was administered by his father, Josiah. (Probate records.)

HENDLEY, CHARLES. Served at Dorchester Heights, March, 1776. Taxed in Medford, 1774 to 1781; occupation, master cooper; came from Boston to Medford.

HOLDEN, DANIEL. Enlisted, 1779, for 9 mos.; age 16; vol. 8, p. 98. Served for Stoneham, 1780; age 17. Son of John and Mary, of Stoneham; born Oct. 15, 1763; married Hannah Green of Pepperill, March 10, 1796; residence at that time, Charlestown.

JACKSON, THOMAS. Enlisted May 21, 1781; age 28; occupation, mariner; vol. 8, p. 690.

KEMP, JOHN. Private, Lexington alarm; served 8 mos., 1775-76; vol. 9, p. 85. Taxed in Medford, 1775.

KENDALL, JONATHAN. Served 1 yr. in Continental Army, from Jan. 1, 1778; in service for Woburn, 1777. Born Sept. 1, 1751; son of Joshua and Esther (Buck); married, Dec. 1, 1774, Joanna Brooks; died in Charlestown, 1795; gravestone.

KING, SAMUEL. Served 6 mos., 1780; age 42; engaged for town of Medfield; residence given Medford. Perhaps an error; vol. 9, p. 270.

LAWRENCE, JONATHAN (Lawrance). Private, Lexington alarm; loaned money to pay bounty, Sept., 1776. Married Mary———; children born in Medford: Jonathan, 1779; Mary, 1780; Jonathan, 1782; William Pitts, 1784. Taxed in Medford, 1772 to 1783; wife admitted to church in Medford from church in Cambridge, 1782; he was admitted to church in Medford, June 10, 1781; died in Ashby, Mass.; will dated May 30, 1817, filed June 26, 1817; widow, Mary, administratrix; only child living, William P., had been an inhabitant of Tennessee for twelve years previous to 1817. (Probate records.)

LeBosquet, Henry. Served 3 yrs., Jackson's Regt., 1777 to 1780; fifer; vol. 9, pp. 402, 621. Son of John and Sarah (Brooks); born Feb. 21, 1763.

LeBosquet, John. Served 3 yrs., Jackson's Regt., 1777-80; artificer; vol. 9, pp. 402, 403, 621. In battles of Bemis Heights and Monmouth; born Dec. 20, 1737; son of Henry and Lydia (Scottow) of Charlestown; married Sarah Brooks, sister of Gov. Brooks; occupation, brazier.

LeBosquet, John, Jr. Fifer; served 3 yrs., Jackson's Regt., 1777-80; vol. 9, pp. 402, 403, 621. Born, 1761; son of John and Sarah (Brooks). At age of 16 he entered the army at Cambridge; he was at Ticonderoga and Valley Forge, and in battles of Bemis Heights and Monmouth. When term of enlistment was over, he went as cabin boy on a merchant vessel which was captured by the British and taken to Halifax. While the captain was alone with the prisoners (the crew having gone ashore for water), the captives overpowered him and started in an open boat for Boston, where they arrived safely. He was in France at the time of the French Revolution. In 1812 he was captain of a vessel, and was taken prisoner and detained in Liverpool over a year. He commanded vessels in East India trade. He married Mary Brooks and lived at her birthplace at Symmes Corner (now Winchester), which was the house where Gov. Brooks was born. For nearly twenty years Capt. LeBosquet was a cripple from paralysis. He died April, 1844, and was buried in his tomb, Salem street, Medford, with military honors. (Luther C. Symmes in *Winchester Press*.)

Leathe, Richard (Leithe). Craft's Co., Greaton's Regt.; reported deserted; age 23; vol. 9, p. 610. Son of John and Elizabeth (Wait); born Nov. 10, 1753. Living in Medford, 1781. His father, who died, 1801, mentions Hannah, daughter of son Richard, deceased. Her guardian was Stephen Dana.

Leithe, John. Served 1 mo. at lines in Boston, 1776; paid money for bounty to men enlisting for Canada, July, 1776, and N. Y., Sept., 1776; vol. 9, pp. 610, 665. Born Oct. 26, 1742; died Oct. 1, 1815; son of John and Elizabeth (Wait). Bequeathed all his property to his brother, Francis; called yeoman; signature, John Leathe.

Manning, Thomas. Served 8 mos., 1775, and guarding troops of convention, 1778; vol. 10, p. 175; served 8 mos., in N. Y., Poor's Regt., 1778-79; corporal; receipt for bounty bears signature; vol. 10, p. 194. Son of Thomas and Sarah (Wyman); born, 1750; married Rebecca Tufts, 1774; residence at that time, Salem; Taxed in Medford, 1776; yeoman.

MANSIR, EBENEZER. Served 8 mos., 1778; receipt for bounty bears signature; vol. 10, p. 203. Son of John of Charlestown, who lived in Medford during the war; born Jan. 6, 1760; married Elizabeth Brown of Boston, Nov. 23, 1781.

MARTEN, FRANCIS. Received bounty from Town of Medford, 1779, for enlisting for 3 mos. (selectmen's order book).

MASON, AARON. 1 mo. service at the lines at Boston, 1776; served 3 yrs., 1777-80, for the Town of Woburn; vol. 10, p. 311. Son of Aaron and Abigail (Reed) of Woburn; born Sept. 27, 1753; died in Woburn, June 3, 1838. "Left no widow or children living." Pensioner. (Probate records.)

McFITEH, JOHN. Enlisted for 3 yrs., 1780; age 23; blacksmith; birthplace Germany; residence Medford; vol. 10, pp. 112, 488.

McLANE, URIAH. Received bounty from Town of Medford for going to N. Y., 1776; residence, Woburn; served 3 yrs., 1777-81; vol. 10, pp. 534 and 538. Son of Charles McLaine of Chelmsford; at age of 17 (March 6, 1767), he chose Samuel Perham guardian. (Probate records.) Name also written Uriah and Uri McLaine.

McNAMAR, PETER or PATRICK. (McNamara, McNamer, McNamor.) Residence Mystic, Medford, and Charlestown; corporal, Hall's Co., Bond's Regt., 1775; Greaton's Regt., 1777-82; vol. 10, pp. 562 and 563. Gave age in 1781, 31 yrs., and in 1818, when he applied for pension, 76 yrs.; residence, 1818, Boston.

MEAD, JOHN. Loaned money to pay bounty to men going to Canada, July, 1776, and to N. Y., Sept., 1776; served before Boston, 1776, and guarding troops of convention, 1778; vol. 10, pp. 580, 584. Son of Israel and Mary; born Feb. 22, 1755; married Katherine Blanchard, May 18, 1786; died July 16, 1812; occupation, tanner.

MITCHELL, PETER. Served at Sewell's Point, 1775; vol. 10, pp. 839 and 851. Enlisted for Canadian Expedition, July, 1776. (Town records.) Taxed in Medford, 1775-76; his wife died in Medford, May 30, 1776.

NOWILL, GEORGE. Served in Continental Army, 1777 to 1781. One George Nowell, son of George and Elizabeth (Whitney), was born in Boston, Sept. 3, 1742.

OAKES, JOHN. Enlisted for 3 yrs., 1777; enlisted for the war, 1779. Born July 12, 1759; son of Edward and Joanna (Griffiths); died Oct. 12, 1799; buried in Salem Street Cemetery.

OSGOOD, DAVID, REV. Chaplain in Stark's N. H. Regt., 1775. Son of Capt. Isaac and Elizabeth (Flint); born in Andover, Mass., Oct. 25, 1747; married Hannah Breed, Nov. 1, 1786; died Dec. 12, 1822; pastor of First Church in Medford, 1773 to 1822; buried in Tomb No. 21, Salem Street Cemetery.

PAIN, RICHARD. Private, Lexington alarm; served at Prospect Hill, 1775; died in service, Aug. 13, 1775. Came to Medford with parents, Stephen and Anna, 1753; came from Amesbury with wife Eunice, Dec. 2, 1765.

PEIRCE, BENJAMIN. Private, Lexington alarm; 8 mos. service, 1775-76. Baptized Dec. 9, 1744; son of Thomas and Sarah (Martin); married Ruth Smith of Woburn, May 24, 1768; taxed 1765 to 1776 in Medford.

PEIRCE, NATHANIEL. Enlisted for Canadian Expedition, 1776; went to Ticonderoga. (Town records.) Served 8 mos., 1775-76; served 9 mos., 1778-79. Pensioner. Son of Nathaniel and Patience (Totman); born Oct. 1, 1750; in Town of Harvard, 1807; died in Medford, July 28, 1821; left widow, Mary.

PEIRCE, RICHARD. Enlisted for the war, 1776; received money due for bounty, May 2, 1785; taxed in Medford, 1785 and '86. Born Jan. 6, 1754; son of Nathaniel and Patience* (Totman); married in Cambridge, Oct. 21, 1784, Anna Dickson (born, 1752); was drowned, Aug. 16, 1797; resided in Medford until 1788, when he removed to Charlestown.

PEIRCE, TITUS. Enlisted for 3 yrs., 1780; age 28; negro.

PEIRCE, WILLIAM. Enlisted, 1775, under Capt. Ebenezer Francis. [William, son of Nathaniel and Patience; born Nov. 16, 1745. William, son of Thomas and Sarah, born July 17, 1747. There is nothing in military or town records to determine whether either of these was the soldier.]

PELHAM, CATO. Enlisted for 3 yrs., 1780; age 30; negro.

PERSON, JAMES (Pierson, Pearson). Served 3 mos. as drummer, 1776. His first wife, Bathshua, died between March 26, 1775, and June 6, 1776; married 2d, Anna Bond, June 6, 1776; [was she widow of Joseph Bond, who died, 1775?]; died Nov. 17, 1790; taxed first in Medford, 1771.

PIKE, BENJAMIN. Served 6 mos., 1778 (archives). Received bounty from Town of Medford, Jan. 5, 1779 (selectmen's order book).

POLLY, ROBERT. Served in R. I. 6 mos., 1777; received bounty from Town of Medford. Probably son of Jacob and Hannah (Scolly) and brother of William, wounded April 19, 1775; born Aug. 11, 1752; taxed in Medford, 1776-77. Robert Polly of New London married Jane Harris of Medford, 1775; of Menotomy, 1781; baptized in Menotomy April 14, 1776; age given then, 22 yrs.; birthplace, Medford; his wife died in Charlestown, 1811; he was living in Medford, April, 1828. Applied for pension, 1818.

*Town records say "Eunice," but she was the wife of Robert Peirce (see church records).

POLLY, WILLIAM. Private, Lexington alarm. Son of Jacob and Hannah (Scolly); born Feb. 2, 1757; died April 25, 1775, from wounds received at Menotomy on the retreat of the British from Concord, April 19.

POLLY, WILLIAM. Enlisted, 1780, for 6 mos.; age 19 (archives). Received bounty for enlisting to go to Clavarack, Oct. 22, 1779 (selectmen's order book). Son of John and Jemima (Nichols); born Oct. 4, 1760; taxed in Medford, 1785.

PORTER, JONATHAN. Commissioned 2d Lieut., July 27, 1776; loaned money to United States Government. Came to Medford from Malden, 1773; proprietor of the Royal Arms Tavern, Medford; land on which it stood is still (1903) in possession of his descendants; son of Dr. Jonathan Porter; married Phebe Abbott of Andover, Nov. 7, 1790; died Nov. 4, 1817; buried in tomb in Salem Street Cemetery.

PRITCHARD, THOMAS. Sergeant, Lexington alarm; served 8 mos., 1775-76, and immediately after the Evacuation of Boston enlisted for the war; commissioned captain, Col. Greaton's Regt.; commended for bravery and fine tactics; sent home as a recruiting officer by Washington, when reënforcements were especially needed. Born in Boston, Aug. 31, 1751; son of William and Atterlante; married Lucy Tufts, daughter of William and Anna (Francis), Feb. 22, 1775; died June 7, 1795, aged 43; occupation, cooper; taxed first in Medford, 1774.

PUTNAM, ELEAZAR. Private, Lexington alarm; 2d Lieut., 1776; served 3 mos. guarding troops of convention, 1778; loaned money for bounty paid to men enlisting for Canada and N. Y., 1776. Came to Medford from Charlestown with wife Mary, 1765; owned covenant in Cambridge Precinct Church (Menotomy), Nov. 24, 1765; born in Danvers, June 5, 1738; son of Henry, mentioned below; died in Medford, Nov. 20, 1804. Family tradition says that one of his sons served as drummer for the Medford company, April 19, 1775, to March 17, 1776. Owned land on High street, Medford.

PUTNAM, HENRY. Killed at Menotomy on retreat of British, April 19, 1775. Served as lieutenant at capture of Louisburg, 1758. Born at Danvers, Mass., Aug. 14, 1712; came to Medford from Charlestown, 1765, with wife Hannah; she died in Newburyport.

PUTNAM, ROGER. Served 1 mo. at lines at Boston, 1776; loaned money to pay bounty to men going to Canada, July, 1776, and to N. Y., Sept., 1776. Son of Henry and Hannah Putnam; taxed first in Medford, 1776; married Sarah Brothers, daughter of Mary, wife of Thomas Richardson (family came from Reading, 1763), Oct. 13, 1774; died Oct. 27, 1794.

RAND, BARRETT. Served at Fort No. 3, 1775; enlisted in 1779 for 9 mos. in Continental service; age 40. Came to Medford 1778 or 1779; taxed, 1780. Son of Joseph and Deborah (Nurs); born Oct. 29, 1738; married Susanna Hopkins, Sept. 15, 1760; died March 1, 1788; occupation, hatter; served as a soldier, 1757; grandfather of Mrs. Lydia Maria Child.

RAND, JACK. Enlisted for 3 yrs., April 27, 1781; age 28; negro. Also served for Woburn, 1777-80.

RAND, NATHANIEL. Served at Fort No. 3, 1775, and guarding troops of convention, 1778. Taxed in Medford, 1776-81. Probably ferryman, of Charlestown; house destroyed, June 17, 1775; took refuge in Medford. Son of Ebenezer and Elizabeth (Brigden); married, 1st, Frances Phillips, March 23, 1743; 2d, Sarah Stacy, June 21, 1759; 3d, Hephzibah Larkin, March 28, 1763; died in Charlestown, Sept. 9, 1795. Had daughter Sarah who served as scout to warn colonists of approach of British before battle of Bunker Hill, and son Nathaniel, Jr., born March 25, 1747, who was taxed in Medford, 1779.

RANSFORD, THOMAS. Loaned money for bounty, Sept., 1776; enlisted for 3 yrs.; return dated, 1778. Served also for Cambridge.

REED, DANIEL. Drummer, Sargent's Regt.; return dated, Oct. 6, 1775; enlisted for 3 yrs. as drum major; return dated, 1778. Son of Seth and Lydia (Cutter); born April 10, 1742; married Dorothy Billings, of Medford, April 12, 1762; died Aug. 22, 1801; belonged to Baptist Church of Menotomy, 1787.

REED, JOSHUA. Enlisted for 3 yrs.; return dated, 1778; Child's Co., Greaton's Regt.

REED, JOSHUA, JR. Private, Hall's Co., 1775; enlisted for Quebec, Sept. 12, 1775. Joshua Reed was taxed in Medford, 1775; possibly these two names refer to the same man. Son of Joshua and Sarah (Dix); born June 29, 1755 (?).

RICE, THOMAS. Enlisted for 3 yrs., 1781; occupation, farmer.

RICHARDSON, ABEL. Private, Lexington alarm. Born in Woburn, Jan. 12, 1750-1; son of Nathan and Mary (Peirce); married Anna Tufts, Dec. 26, 1775; died Sept., 1824; aged 74; taxed in Medford, 1774 and 1775; taxed in Woburn, 1776 to 1780.

RICHARDSON, JAMES, JR. Private, Hall's Co., Prospect Hill, 1775. Probably of Woburn; not taxed in Medford.

ROBBINS, NATHANIEL. Served before Boston, 1776; probably served as substitute, as a boy too young for regular military service might work building fortifications; no other service recorded. Son of

Thomas and Sarah (Gould); born May 16, 1762; came to Medford from Cambridge with parents, Dec. 3, 1764; his father was taxed in Medford, 1764 to 1774.

ROUSE, BENJAMIN. Loaned money for bounty, July, 1776, and Sept., 1776; served guarding troops of convention, 1778. Taxed in Medford, 1769 to 1790; married Elizabeth French, April 13, 1769; died June 25, 1797; a veteran of French and Indian War.

ROYALL, SAM. Enlisted Nov., 1780, for the war.

RUMRILL, ABNER. Served 8 mos. at Prospect Hill, 1775; also in service, 1777, '78, and '79. Born in Medford, March 15, 1755; son of John and Mary (Peirce) of Charlestown, who were married, 1749; married in Newton, Sept. 30, 1779, Sally Binford.

RUMRILL, ISAAC. Served 8 mos. at Prospect Hill, 1775; son of John and Mary, born June 25, 1757. John, the father of these two men, was born in Old Dunstable about 1721, and died Jan. 29, 1763; he served in the French and Indian War.

SARGENT, ABEL. Residence, Medford; enlisted for Templeton for 3 yrs; return dated, 1778.

SARGENT, REUBEN. Served in R. I., 1777; enlisted for 3 yrs., July 9, 1777; residence, Medford; enlisted for Woburn.

SASON (?), WILLIAM. Enlisted for 3 yrs., 1782; signature on receipt.

SAVELS, BENJAMIN. Private, Lexington alarm; served 8 mos. at Prospect Hill, 1775-76. Came from Cambridge to Medford, 1764.

SAVELS, THOMAS. Private, Lexington alarm; served 8 mos. at Prospect Hill, 1775-76; sergeant; enlisted for 3 yrs., 1777; reënlisted for 6 mos., 1780; age 30. Son of Joseph, Jr., and Martha (Prior) Sables or Savels, who came from Boston to Medford, Feb. 8, 1758; married Miriam Royall, Dec. 23, 1773; died in Medford, April 30, 1801, aged 51; buried in Salem Street Cemetery; name written Sables on tombstone.

SECCOMB, FRANCIS. Enlisted for 3 yrs.; return dated, 1778; negro.

SIMONDS, JOSHUA. Corporal; served guarding troops of convention, 1778. Son of Joshua and Rebecca ———; born March 18, 1758; married Abigail Tufts, Nov. 24, 1779; died Feb. 20, 1833; lived in house on Simonds Hill, High street.

SIMONDS, ———. Two men served at Dorchester Heights, March, 1776. Probably Joshua (above) and Jude (see civil list).

SKILLINGS, POLLADOR (Polledore Skinnings). Enlisted April 2, 1781; age 19; negro. Lived in Charlestown, 1803.

SMITH, JOHN. Private, Lexington alarm; served 8 mos. at Prospect Hill, 1775. Taxed in Medford, 1773 to 1782; son of John and Abigail (Stratton); born Aug. 12, 1743; married Oct. 26, 1763, Mrs. Mary Whitney; joined 2d Precinct Church, Woburn, 1764; came to Medford from Woburn, 1773.

SMITH, WILLIAM. Enlisted for 1 yr., Jan. 1, 1778; passed muster at Concord, July 22, 177—.

STEWARD, AMASA. Enlisted for 3 yrs., May 16, 1782; signature on receipt. Bounty paid to Jeremiah (see treasurer's records). One Jeremiah Steward or Stewart was taxed in Medford, 1778, '79, and '80; had seat in Cambridge N. W. Precinct meeting house, 1781.

STICKNEY, BENJAMIN. Fifer; served 1 yr. from Jan., 1778; passed muster, July 22, 177—; signature on original papers in Mass. archives. Benj. Stickney, born in Byfield, was a fifer in another regiment at this time. This man may been the Benjamin born in Hampton, N. H., Feb. 5, 1744, who served in French war and died at sea, unmarried.

SYMMES, JOHN. Served 8 mos. at Prospect Hill, 1775-76 (archives); at battle of Bunker Hill; served 5 mos. in Wheelock's Regt., 1776. Private Gerrish's Regt., 1777; (pension records). Enlisted for 3 yrs., 1777; spent one winter at Ticonderoga *(Symmes Memorial)*. He was a wheelwright and blacksmith at Symmes Corner, Medford (now Winchester); son of John and Abigail (Dix); born Aug. 16, 1755; married Elizabeth Wright, Oct. 31, 1780 (marriage fee, $100); died June 24, 1834; buried in Oak Grove Cemetery, Medford.

SYMMES, JOSIAH. Served 1 mo. at lines in Boston, 1776. Son of John and Abigail (Dix); baptized Sept. 3, 1758; married Elizabeth Johnson; he was over 50 when he married; died about 1828.

SYMMES, ZECHARIAH. Served 3 mos. guarding troops of convention, 1778; loaned money for bounty paid to soldiers going to N. Y., Sept., 1776; loaned money to United States Government. Son of Zechariah and Judith (Eames); born in Woburn, now Winchester, Oct. 1, 1744; married Rebecca Tuttle. His father left him a handsome property in 1793, and he then became the proprietor of the Black Horse Tavern, just over the old Medford line. Taxed in Medford, 1778 to 1785; he and his wife were admitted to Church in Medford, Jan. 26, 1776.

TEALL, SAMUEL (Teel). 2d Lieut. Dorchester Heights, March, 1776. Born 1749; son of Samuel and Jane (Dickson); baptized 1755; married Ruth Walker, Nov. 5, 1772; died Feb. 25, 1832; aged 83; buried in Tomb No. 17, Salem Street Cemetery.

TEEL, GERSHOM. Corporal, Lexington alarm; served 8 mos. at Prospect Hill, 1775-76. Born in Charlestown; son of Samuel and Jane (Dickson); baptized June 29, 1755; married Susanna Adams, Oct. 3, 1776; died Dec. 8, 1822; taxed in Medford, 1776, '82 and '83; of Lunenburg, 1777. Samuel Teel, his son, who died in Medford, 1861, was born in Lunenburg, 1778. Children baptized in Menotomy, 1788 and 1791.

THOMPSON, EBENEZER. Served guarding troops of convention, 1778; loaned money for bounty, Sept., 1776. Married, 1st, Esther ———, who died May 26, 1777; aged 23; 2d, May 21, 1778, Katherine Greenleaf, daughter of Gardiner; she was born 1756, and died Sept. 22, 1793; married, 3d, Hannah Tufts, Nov. 20, 1794; she died, 1836; aged 80; he died March 5, 1800; taxed first in Medford, 1776.

TORRY, THOMAS. Enlisted for 3 yrs., 1781; occupation, farmer; age 21; negro.

TUFTS, AARON. Enlisted for 3 yrs., return dated Feb., 1778; enlisted for 8 mos., 1780; age 19. Son of William and Susanna; born Dec. 18, 1761. Probably Aaron, who died in Old Mill Prison, England, Sept. 18, 1781.

TUFTS, BENJAMIN. Served guarding troops of convention at Cambridge, 1778; loaned money to pay bounty July and Sept., 1776. Son of Benjamin and Mary (Hutchinson), born Nov. 15, 1731; married, 1st, Esther Lynde; 2d, Lydia Francis; died Jan. 14, 1804; aged 73; buried in Salem Street Cemetery.

TUFTS, CALEB. Served 3 mos., 1776. Taxed in Medford, 1785; son of Samuel and Hannah (Tufts); born Sept. 5, 1762; married, 1787, Rebecca Burrows; settled in Mystic, Conn.; died in Mystic, 1852; occupation, brick-layer and farmer.

TUFTS, CATO (Turfts). Served at Bunker Hill, Prescott's Regt.; in service, Oct., 1775.

TUFTS, DANIEL. Private, Lexington alarm; worked with team at Dorchester Heights, March, 1776; 2d lieut. of militia, 1781; loaned money to pay bounty, Sept., 1776. Born, 1753; son of Nathan and Mary (Adams); married Abigail Tufts, sister of Benjamin, mentioned above, June 12, 1775; died in Charlestown, Mass., April 27, 1839; buried in Phipps Street Cemetery, Charlestown; lived near Powder House, Somerville; land where his house stood set off from Medford to Charlestown, 1811.

TUFTS, DAVID. Served guarding troops of convention, 1778; joined Continental Army at Clavarack, 1779. Enlisted for Billerica for 3 yrs., 1781. Son of William and Mary (Francis); born June 17, 1763; died July 6, 1823, in Lynn; married, 1st, Mary Massey; 2d, Elizabeth Mansfield; 3d, Eunice Hart. First regular express driver in Lynn;

kept a hotel corner Federal street and Market Square, Lynn. Ancestor of Col. Gardiner Tufts.

TUFTS, EBENEZER. Private, Lexington alarm; served guarding troops of convention, 1778; at Noddle's Island, 1776; loaned money to pay bounty to men going to N. Y., Sept., 1776. Son of James; born, 1737; married Abigail Cook, April 23, 1760; died Feb. 26, 1809; buried in Salem Street Cemetery. Taxed in Medford, 1757 to 1802, also 1806, '07, and '08.

TUFTS, EBENEZER. Enlisted for 1 yr., 1776; was in battle of Trenton; also served in R. I., 1780, in Col. Cyprian How's Regt. Son of William (noted for bravery at siege of Louisburg), and Catherine (Tufts); born, 1761; married, 1st, Hannah Levistone, 1781; 2d, Elizabeth Traverse, 1802. He was a nephew of Lieut. Moses Tufts, his mother's brother. Pensioner.

TUFTS, FRANCIS.* Enlisted for Canada, July, 1776; went as far as Ticonderoga. (Town records.) Served in Continental Army 3 yrs.; promoted several times; distinguished himself at Saratoga; his orderly book was forwarded to the Pension Department, but never returned. He was born in Lancaster, Mass., son of William and Mary (Francis) of Medford, 1756; married Hannah Greenleaf, June 12, 1775; died Aug. 18, 1823; occupation, distiller.

TUFTS, GEORGE. Loaned money to pay bounty, July and Sept., 1776; enlisted for 3 yrs., 1777; reported deserted; was at home, sick, Dec. 10, 1780. Son of William and Catherine (Wyman); married Elizabeth Hartwell, 1767; married, 2d, Mary ———, who survived him; died Aug. 25, 1796.

TUFTS, ISSAC. Sergeant, Lexington alarm; at Dorchester Heights, March 1776; loaned money for bounty paid to men going to N. Y., Sept., 1776; loaned money to United States Government. Born 1744; son of James and Lydia (Hall); died 1823; married Martha C. Frost April 16, 1769. Lived on College Hill, then called Walnut Hill, near site of Tufts College.

TUFTS, JAMES, JR. Private, Lexington alarm; served 8 mos., 1775-76; loaned money for bounty, July and Sept., 1776. Son of James and Tabitha (Binford); born 1755; married Elizabeth Hay; died 1810. With son James he kept a public house, and afterward had a pottery on south side of Mystic river, just off of Main street; property taken for Mystic River Reservation, 1900; buried in Salem Street Cemetery.

*Promoted to ensign at Saratoga by Gen. Gates. Brooks' History incorrect. See text.

TUFTS, JOHN. Corporal, Lexington alarm; served 8 mos., 1775-76. Son of Peter and Anne (Adams); born 1754-5; married Elizabeth Perry; died Sept. 10, 1839; lived on Sycamore street, Somerville, in house now (1903) occupied by Somerville Historical Society, Lee's Headquarters, 1775.

TUFTS, JONATHAN. Private, Lexington alarm; served at lines in Boston, 1776. Born, 1739; son of James and Lydia (Hall); married Elizabeth Holden before 1764; died Sept. 26, 1784; buried in Salem Street Cemetery.

TUFTS, MOSES. 1st Lieut. Hall's Co. at Dorchester Heights, March, 1776 (archives). Went on Canadian Expedition, July, 1776 (town records). Schoolmaster in Medford; son of William and Catherine (Wyman); baptized Oct. 7, 1744; married Phebe Thompson, 1767. Lived on Salem street nearly opposite Ashland street.

TUFTS, NATHAN, JR. Loaned money to pay bounty, Sept., 1776; served guarding troops of convention, 1778. Son of William and Susanna; born, 1750; married Sarah Trefrey Feb. 22, 1776; died March, 1819.

TUFTS, PETER, JR. Private, Lexington alarm; loaned money for bounty paid to men enlisting July and Sept., 1776; served guarding troops of convention, 1778. Son of Peter and Anne (Adams) of Winter Hill; born 1753; married Hannah Adams; died 1836. Lived in house occupied at one time by his cousin Daniel, opposite Powder House; through his influence his homestead lot was set off to Charlestown in 1811.

TUFTS, SAMUEL. Private, Lexington alarm; loaned money to pay bounty July, 1776 (archives). Committee of safety, 1779 (town records). Son of Joseph and Lydia (Francis); born Aug. 16, 1732; married Hannah Tufts; died 1818; aged 86; gravestone, Salem Street Cemetery.

TUFTS, SAMUEL. Private, Walton's Co. at Noddle's Island, 1776; wages paid to his father, Joseph Tufts. Born 1759 or 1760; his mother's name was Hannah; married Martha Upham; died in Westford, 1818 or 1819; occupation, dyer.

TUFTS, SAMUEL. Enlisted in King's Co., Marshall's Regt., April 13, 1777; transferred to Invalid Corps, May, 1779; corporal, Turner's Co., Tupper's Regt., 1781; age 24. Received $20 for military service, Jan. 18, 1802. Born Feb. 21, 1758; son of Ichabod and Rebecca (Francis); married Mary ———; had children born in Boston.

TUFTS, SAMUEL. Enlisted, 1780, for 6 mos.; age 19. Son of Samuel and Hannah (Tufts); born April, 1761; taxed 1781.

TUFTS, SAMUEL, 3D. Private, Lexington alarm; paid money for bounty to men going to N. Y. (Called Jr., 1776.) Born 1752; son of William and Mary (Francis); married Margaret Hodgkins of Ipswich before 1779; died Nov. 20, 1815; gravestone in Salem Street Cemetery.

TUFTS, WILLIAM. Served at lines at Boston, 1776; in Col. Wesson's Regt., 1777. Son of William and Catherine (Tufts); born 1762; killed 1777.

TUFTS, WILLIAM, 4TH. Joined army at Clavarack, 1779, for 3 mos.; signature on original receipt for bounty in archives.

TUTTLE, ADAM. Enlisted for 3 yrs., April, 1781; age 22; occupation, farmer; negro.

TYLER, MOSES. Served in R. I., 1779, 6 mos. (archives and selectmen's order book). He also served 6 mos. in 1776, and 6 mos., 1780; was at battle of Yorktown (pension papers). Son of Moses and Eleanor; born 1757, in Woburn; married Anna (Kendall) Monroe June 28, 1770; residence probably Woburn. After the war went to Lunenburg; in 1832 a resident of Harvard; age 74.

TYSSICK, JOSEPH. In Brooks' Co., Thatcher's Regt., 1778; age 20. Son of Ralph and Rebecca (Myrick); born May 10, 1758; died Sept. 19, 1813; came to Medford from Charlestown with his mother, 1775; married Isabel Winship Sept. 20, 1784; taxed in Medford 1780 to 1803, except 1793, '96 and '97.

TYSSICK, SAMUEL. Enlisted for 6 mos., 1780; age 18; born Feb. 28, 1762. Son of Ralph and Rebecca (Myrick); brother of Joseph; came to Medford, 1775.

VERDER, SAMUEL. Enlisted for 3 yrs., 1777. Married, 1st, Hannah ———— (family tradition). Came to Medford with wife Beulah and children, Hannah and Elizabeth, from " Newtown," 1766; Mrs. Verder died Oct. 25, 1782; married Phebe Dexter, April 30, 1783; died Dec. 22, 1793.

VINTON, DAVID. Private, Lexington alarm; served on Privateer, *True Blue*, which captured a British snow. Vinton was put on board as one of a prize crew; the snow was recaptured, and Vinton was carried a prisoner to Halifax; exchanged June 28, 1777. He enlisted again on brigantine, *Hazard;* served from Oct. 23, 1777 to May 20, 1778. Died in Medford Dec. 3, 1778; aged 32; buried in Salem Street Cemetery; his wife, Mary Gowen, daughter of Hammond, and a child six weeks old, died Sept., 1775.

WADE, JAMES. Sergeant at Prospect Hill, 1775. Son of Samuel Wade; born 1750; married Mary, daughter of Rev. Edward Upham of Newport. His father owned land where the Fountain House stood, Salem street.

WAIT, DARIUS. Served at lines at Boston, 1776 (archives). Received bounty for going to Ticonderoga, 1776 (selectmen's order book). Same as Uriah Wait in petition for bounty, town records, vol. 3. Born April 9, 1757; son of Timothy and Joanna.

WAIT, JACOB. Loaned money for bounty, July, 1776. Received bounty for enlisting in army (selectmen's order book, Feb. 17, 1777). Taxed in Medford, 1781; born June 5, 1759; son of Timothy and Joanna; occupation in 1789, glazier; died Jan. 23, 1801.

WAIT, TIMOTHY. Served in army 6 mos., 1778 (selectmen's order book, July 18, Sept. 23 and Dec. 23, 1778). Born April 1, 1761; son of Timothy and Joanna.

WAKEFIELD, THOMAS. Private, Lexington alarm; at Prospect Hill, 1775; received money for bounty coat, Jan. 8, 1776. Son of Samuel and Elizabeth; born Nov. 10, 1756; died Jan. 28, 1776.

WARREN (see Woren).

WARREN, THOMAS. Enlisted for 3 yrs., Poor's New Hampshire Regt., return dated Feb., 1778. Son of Dea. Isaac and Elizabeth (Reeves); born Dec. 21, 1755.

WATSON, ISAAC. Private, Lexington alarm; paid money to men going to Canada, July, 1776. Son of Isaac and Elizabeth (Whittemore); baptized Oct. 30, 1748; married Ruth Locke Sept. 26, 1771; occupation, saddler; owned land near Highland avenue and High street; taxed in Medford, 1774 to 1797.

WHITMORE, FRANCIS. Served at lines in Boston, 1776; loaned money for bounty, July and Sept., 1776. Taxed in Medford, 1766 to 1792; son of Capt. Francis and Mary (Hall); born Aug. 16, 1741; he was the last of the family name to reside permanently in Medford; married Elizabeth Bowman Dec. 30, 1764, at Menotomy. He was in business with his father "on the Kennebec" in 1770.

WHITEMORE, JOHN. At Prospect Hill, 1775. Probably son of Capt. Francis *Whitmore* and Mary (Hall); born Nov. 25, 1754.

WILKINS, AMOS. Enlisted for 3 yrs., April, 1781; occupation, farmer; age 17.

SOLDIERS AND SAILORS CREDITED TO MEDFORD. 55

WILLEY, NATHAN. Served in R. I., 1779; taxed in Medford, 1790 to 1793; born in Stoneham, Jan. 1, 1756; son of James and Hannah (Hay). He was born in the south part of town, near Spot Pond; married Priscilla Hadley. While in Medford they lived opposite the junction of Fulton and Highland streets; house was burned, 1842. He died 1799.

WILLIAMS, JOHN. Served at Prospect Hill 1775 and 1776. [Name appears on tax list 1764 to 1771. In 1774 Rachel Williams, widow of John, sold her property on Salem street, nearly opposite the present site of Mystic Church. Possibly John and Rachel were parents of this soldier. Rachel died, 1785, and bequeathed property to John Williams, her grandchild, also son Ebenezer and several daughters.]

WILLSON, ANDREW. Corporal; served in R. I., 1777. Andrew and Joanna (Winship) of Menotomy were married July 5, 1757, and a son, Andrew, was baptized May 28, 1758.

WILSON, JOSEPH. Served at lines at Boston, 1776, and 6 mos., 1778. Taxed in Medford, 1780, '81, '82. Probably son of Edward Wilson of Menotomy and Lucy Francis of Medford; baptized Oct. 28, 1759; married Elizabeth Caldwell, March 6, 1785.

WOREN, SAMUEL. Enlisted for 3 yrs., 1782.

WYMAN, JAMES. Served at Prospect Hill, 1775. Son of James Wyman, town treasurer, and Susanna (Cutter); born Jan. 21, 1757; married, 1st, Mehitabel (Bacon?); 2d, Mary Gill, 1817; occupation, carpenter; Went to Keene, N. H.

YEARNEY, SAMPSON. Enlisted for Canadian Expedition, July, 1776 (town records). Enlisted for Town of Concord, 1777; residence Medford; free negro. Name written Orney, Yarnee, and Yarner. Son of Sampson and Hannah (Anthony), who were married March 16, 1747. Sampson, Sr., was a slave of Peter Seccomb, who died 1756. After his master's death, Sampson bought his time and was made free. The wife of Sampson, the soldier, became the wife of John Greenough, the village fiddler.

PATRIOTIC CITIZENS.

THE FOLLOWING LIST IS MADE UP OF CIVIL OFFICERS AND OTHERS, NOT SOLDIERS, WHO AIDED THE CAUSE OF FREEDOM BY LOANS TO TOWN, STATE OR NATIONAL GOVERNMENT.

ANGIER, ABIGAIL, widow. Loaned money to United States Government. Born Abigail Watson, daughter of Jonathan and Abigail (Bradshaw); baptized Nov. 2, 1729; married Samuel Angier, April 29, 1762. He died Aug. 22, 1775; aged 53; he was a graduate of Harvard, 1748; taught school in Medford and preached for several years, but was probably never ordained. Mrs. Angier was taxed in Medford 1775 to 1779.

BACON, SAMUEL. Loaned money to pay bounty to men enlisting for N. Y., Sept., 1776. Married Anna Mead Nov. 29, 1759; died Feb. 12, 1778; taxed first in Medford, 1758.

BISHOP, JOHN. Loaned money to United States Government. Committee of advice "to advise with any of the neighboring towns . . . and for to Endeavor to keep pease and good order in this Town," Sept. 25, 1774. Son of Dr. John Bishop, who came to Medford, 1685, and Sarah———; born 1722; married Abigail, daughter of Dr. Simon Tufts, Sr., Dec. 7, 1752; died Dec. 17, 1791; home on High street, West Medford; taxed first in Medford, 1743.

BLANCHARD, SAMUEL. Loaned money to pay bounty to men enlisting for Canadian Expedition, July, 1776. Son of Samuel and Sarah Pratt; born Feb. 1, 1720 (birth recorded in Malden); lived in that part of Medford now called Wellington; married Sarah Cutter April 12, 1745; died Sept. 1, 1790; had eight children born in Malden, and one in Medford; taxed in Medford, 1765 to 1785.

BLODGETT, JONATHAN. Loaned money to pay bounty to men enlisting to go to Canada, July, 1776. Son of Seth and Elizabeth (Harding); born in Woburn April 29, 1743; taxed in Medford, 1775, '76,' 77, '78, '79.

BLODGETT, SETH, CAPT. Loaned money to pay bounty, July, 1776. Son of Caleb and Sarah (Wyman) of Woburn; born Feb. 2, 1718-9; married Elizabeth Harding; proprietor of mill at foot of Cross street, Medford, 1761 to 1780; died Oct. 8, 1783; member of Ancient and Honorable Artillery; taxed in Medford from 1751 to 1783, except 1765, '66, '67, and '70.

BRADSHAW, SIMON. Loaned money for bounty, July, 1776. Leather dresser; born March 5, 1739; son of Simon and Mary (Johnson); married Hannah Johnson July 12, 1770; taxed 1760 to 1777 in Medford.

BRADSHAW, WILLIAM. Loaned money for bounty, July, 1776. Born Aug. 14, 1733; son of Jonathan and Mary (Watson); married Elizabeth Lampson, June 5, 1761; died in Medford April 8, 1793; taxed first in Medford, 1754.

BROOKS, ABIGAIL. Served chocolate to soldiers passing her house returning from battle of Lexington. Born Abigail Brown, daughter of Rev. John of Haverhill and Joanna (Cotton), a descendant of Rev. John Cotton; married Rev. Edward Brooks; died Nov. 28, 1800; aged 69.

BROOKS, EBENEZER, JR., CAPT. Committee of correspondence, 1775; committee of advice, 1774. Son of Caleb and Mary (Wyer); married Susanna Thompson, daughter of Thomas and Sarah (Bradshaw); died Sept. 18, 1775; aged 40; half brother of Gov. John Brooks; taxed 1757-1774.

BROOKS, THOMAS. Loaned money for bounty paid men enlisting to go to N. Y., Sept., 1776; loaned money to town for military purposes; representative to General Court, 1776 to 1782. Born Jan. 6, 1732; son of Samuel and Mary (Boutwell); married, 1st, Feb. 27, 1755, Anna Hall; 2d, Mercy, daughter of Dr. Simon Tufts, Sr., 1762; died March 7, 1799. Grandfather of Rev. Charles Brooks, who wrote *History of Medford*.

BURNS, FRANCIS. Loaned money for bounty, July, 1776. Trader; taxed first in Medford, 1751; married, 1st, Margaret McClelland or McKlennin; 2d, Hannah Brooks, daughter of Caleb and Ruth Albree, 1794; died Dec. 5, 1800; aged 77. Mary, 1st wife of Samuel Buel, was his daughter by first wife.

CODMAN, ISAAC. Loaned money to United States Government. "Late inhabitant of Charlestown, 1775"; taxed in Medford, 1775 to 1782, inclusive; son of John and Parnell (Foster); baptized Aug. 21, 1737; married Abigail Foster, Sept. 22, 1768; served as a soldier, 1757; left no children. (Wyman.)

FOSTER, JONATHAN. Loaned money for bounty, July, 1776; chairman of a "class" for recruiting, 1782. Married Susanna Tufts, March 19, 1776; wife admitted to church in Medford, June 16, 1776; taxed in Medford, 1774 to 1778; in Boston, 1788 to 1793; living in 1813.

FOWLE, HENRY. Loaned money to United States Government; committee of prosecution, 1777; loaned money for bounty paid men enlisting to go to Canada, July, 1776, and N. Y., Sept., 1776. Son of Henry and Dorothy (Seccomb); born March 15, 1741; married Mary Patten, Jan. 8, 1766; owned land on High street, east of Governor's avenue; died June 13, 1810.

FRANCIS, SETH. Loaned money for bounty, July, 1776. Born Jan. 14, 1744; son of Stephen and Love, widow of Josiah Wyman and daughter of Lieut. Seth and Esther (Johnson) Wyman; died Oct. 31, 1791.

FROTHINGHAM, JOSEPH. Loaned money to United States Government. Probably son of Nathaniel and Susanna (Whittemore); born Jan. 15, 1723-4; married, 1st, Mary Foster, 1750, and 2d, Deborah Rand, 1752; died Sept. 21, 1787 (Wyman). Taxed in Medford, 1778 to 1783, inclusive.

FULTON, JOHN. Loaned money for bounty paid to men enlisting July, 1776 and Sept., 1776. Born in Boston; probably son of John and Ann Wier; married Sarah Bradlee, 1767; came to Medford from Boston, 1772; died Feb. 9, 1790; occupation, bookkeeper.

FULTON, SARAH. Carried despatches to Boston during siege by order of Gen. Washington; nursed wounded soldiers in field hospital at Medford, after battle of Bunker Hill; assisted in disguising her husband and brothers for " Boston Tea Party." Fulton street, Medford, named in her honor. Daughter of Samuel and Mary (Andrus) Bradlee; born in Dorchester, Dec. 24, 1740; died Nov. 13, 1835; wife of John Fulton mentioned above.

GOWEN, WILLIAM. Loaned money to United States Government for military purposes; one of committee to settle bounty accounts, 1778; loaned money for bounty paid to men enlisting to go to N. Y., Sept., 1776. Son of Hammond and Mary (Crosswell) of Charlestown; baptized Sept. 13, 1749; married Eleanor Cutter, daughter of Ebenezer, April 29, 1772; father of Maria Gowen Brooks, the novelist; taxed in Medford, 1771 to 1794.

GREENLEAF, GARDINER. Loaned money for bounty, July, 1776. Son of Stephen and Mary; born Jan. 9, 1726; married Catherine Thompson Jan. 21, 1748; died Nov. 21, 1808.

HALL, AARON, A.M. Loaned money for bounty, July, 1776; representative to General Court, 1772-75, and 1782-84. Son of Hon. Stephen Hall and Mary (Muzzy); born April 23, 1737; married Rebecca Pool, Jan. 3, 1760; died March 19, 1787.

HALL, BENJAMIN. Representative to General Court, 1770 to 1773; member of Provincial Congress, 1774-75; committee of correspondence, 1775; committee of safety, 1777; loaned money to Town of Medford for bounty, and to United States Government for military purposes. Son of Andrew and Abigail (Walker); born Jan. 27, 1731; married, 1st, Hepzibah Jones, May 3, 1753; 2d, Mary Green (widow), Aug. 23, 1791; died Feb. 2, 1817; occupation, distiller and general trader. For further account of his life see *Medford Historical Register*, vol. 3, p. 76.

HALL, BENJAMIN, JR. Loaned money to pay bounty to those enlisting to go to Canada, July, 1776, and to go to N. Y., Sept., 1776; town clerk, 1783. Son of Benjamin and Hepzibah (Jones); born Aug. 9, 1754; married Lucy Tufts, daughter of Dr. Simon and Lucy (Dudley), Nov. 20, 1777; died Sept. 19, 1807; he began housekeeping in the "Jonathan Wade," or "Garrison House," but from 1785 to his death lived in house on easterly corner of High street and Governor's avenue.

HALL, EBENEZER, CAPT. Committee of correspondence, 1776; committee of prosecution, 1777; committee of safety, 1777; on various committees of patriotic nature during war. Son of John and Elizabeth (Walker); baptized July 24, 1737; married Susanna Floyd, Nov. 3, 1763; died May 1, 1800; called " Baker Hall."

HALL, EBENEZER, JR. Loaned money for bounty, Sept., 1776. Son of Andrew and Abigail (Walker); born May 31, 1748; married Martha Jones April 12, 1770; died March 21, 1835; occupation, tanner; residence High street, between Governor's avenue and Bradlee road.

HALL, FITCH. Loaned money for bounty, Sept., 1776. Son of Benjamin and Hepzibah (Jones); born Jan. 27, 1759; married Judith Brasher May 14, 1783; died Dec. 28, 1841; occupation, distiller.

HALL, RICHARD. Committee of safety, 1777; loaned money to United States Government for military purposes; town clerk; loaned large sums to town for army expenses. Born Nov. 12, 1737; son of Andrew and Abigail (Walker); married Lucy Jones, sister of wives of Benjamin and Ebenezer Hall, Jr., Nov. 9, 1762; died June 27, 1827; occupation, hatter; lived in house on westerly corner of High street and Governor's avenue.

HALL, SAMUEL. Loaned money to United States Government for military purposes; committee of safety, 1780, '81. Son of Jonathan and Anna (Fowle); born Nov. 2, 1740; died Oct. 10, 1807; called " Printer

Hall"; published *Salem Gazette*, 1768-74; established *New England Chronicle*, 1775, in Cambridge; removed business to Boston, 1776; published *Salem Gazette*, 1781, and *Massachusetts Gazette*, 1785; in 1789, he opened a book-store in Boston; taxed in Medford, 1774, and from 1776 to 1800.

HALL, STEPHEN, ESQ. Chosen to meet with committee of convention, 1768, at Boston; representative to General Court, 1763 to 1770; committee of advice, 1774; loaned money for bounty, July, 1776. Son of Capt. John and Jemima (Syll); born Jan. 19, 1704; married Mary Muzzy, Dec. 14, 1732; he was called "Jr." because he had an uncle, Stephen Hall, living in Medford; also called "Honorable" and "Gentleman"; died Dec. 1, 1786.

HALL, STEPHEN, TERTIUS. Committee of correspondence, 1773, '75, '76; committee of advice, 1774; committee of prosecution, 1777; committee of safety, 1777, '78, '79; representative to Provincial Congress, 1775. Born Aug. 10, 1721; married Sarah Keizar, Jan. 5, 1743 (parish records); died Aug. 12 (?), 1796.

HALL, WILLIS. Committee of advice, 1774; loaned money for bounty, July and Sept., 1776. Son of Hon. Stephen and Mary (Muzzy); born Aug. 20, 1733; died Dec. 3, 1812; married Sarah Holmes, Nov. 11, 1790; he was grandfather of Maj. George L. Stearns, who organized negro regiments during the Civil War.

KIDDER, SAMUEL, DEACON. Committee of advice, 1774; committee of correspondence, 1775-76. Born in Cambridge, June 21, 1720; son of Francis and Mary (Prentice); married, 1st, Mary Thompson, March 20, 1744; 2d, Joanna ———; died March 6, 1777; aged 57; lived on Salem street, near River street; taxed first in Medford, 1741.

LEATHE, JOHN. Loaned money to United States Government for war purposes; loaned money to pay bounty, July, 1776. Occupation, cordwainer; taxed first in Medford, 1739; married Elizabeth Waite, Nov. 10, 1741; died Jan. 16, 1801; aged 83; heirs, John, Francis, Sarah, and Hannah, daughter of Richard deceased.

MEAD, ISRAEL. Loaned money to pay bounty, July, 1776. Came to Medford from Watertown, with wife and three children, May 3, 1756; taxed in Medford, 1757 to 1779; occupation, tailor; born in Watertown, Aug. 27, 1716; son of John and Rebecca; wife, Mary ———; died Aug. 25, 1795.

NEWHALL, TIMOTHY. Committee of prosecution, 1777. Loaned money for bounty, July and Sept., 1776. Married Susanna Bradshaw (born May, 1742), daughter of Jonathan and Mary, March 1, 1764; she died May 27, 1776; aged 34 (tombstone); he died Jan. 14, 1799; taxed in Medford, 1761 to 1799.

PATTEN, JONATHAN. Committee of safety, 1778-79; town treasurer, 1778 to 1786; loaned money for bounty, July, 1776; loaned money to United States Government to carry on the war. Son of William and Anna (Seccomb); born July 7, 1738; married Susanna Bradshaw (born July 12, 1741; died, 1833), daughter of Stephen and Mary, April 14, 1762; died July 28, 1790; taxed first in Medford, 1759.

PATTEN, THOMAS. Committee of advice, 1774; loaned money to United States Government; committee of correspondence, 1775; loaned money to pay bounty, July, 1776. Born Feb. 20, 1719; son of William and Abigail, daughter of Stephen Willis; married, 1st., Mary, daughter of Jonathan Tufts, innholder, and Sarah (Wait), Jan. 10, 1745; married, 2d, Mary Binford, Jan. 8, 1765; died Nov. 26, 1786; called brickmaker and yeoman; taxed first in Medford, 1740; uncle of Jonathan, above.

PEIRCE, JOSEPH. Loaned money to pay bounty, July, 1776. Son of Nathaniel; baptized March 20, 1742; married Hannah Sockers, Nov. 6, 1771; died Aug. 18, 1777.

POLLY, NATHANIEL. Loaned money for bounty, July, 1776. Son of Samuel and Elizabeth ———; born April 27, 1731; married Mary ———; died April 27, 1796. His house stood corner of Salem street and Revere place; it was moved to the end of the court and was standing in 1880. (J. H. Hooper, a descendant.)

POOL, RICHARD. Loaned money for bounty, July and Sept., 1776. Born April 13, 1756; son of Zachariah and Rebecca (Wade); married Frances Calf (Calef), Oct. 1, 1778; died Dec. 9, 1781.

SIMONDS, JOSHUA. Committee of correspondence, 1773 and 1776; committee of advice, 1774; committee of safety, 1777; loaned money to United States Government; selectman during war; loaned money to pay bounty July and Sept., 1776. Married Rebecca ———, before 1747; died Jan. 7, 1793; taxed first in Medford, 1746.

SIMONDS, JUDE. Loaned money for bounty, July and Sept., 1776. Married Elizabeth Polly, Nov. 10, 1772; taxed in Medford, 1771-1805.

SYMMES, JOHN. Loaned money for bounty, July and Sept., 1776. Son of William and Ruth (Converse); born 1720; married Nov. 7, 1754, Abigail Dix of Waltham; died between Jan. 1 and Dec. 1, 1785; lived in what is now Winchester.

SYMMES, TIMOTHY. Loaned money for bounty, July, 1776. Born 1714; son of William and Ruth (Converse); married Elizabeth Bodge; died Oct. 30, 1783; taxed in Medford, 1754 to Sept., 1783.

TEEL, BENJAMIN. Loaned money to United States Government; loaned money for bounty, July, 1776. Son of Benjamin of Charlestown (now West Somerville) and Anna (Jenkins); born July 1, 1719; married Mary Gill of Malden, April 7, 1783; died Aug. 25, 1784; left the bulk of his property to Jonathan and Benjamin Teel, his nephews.

THOMPSON, JOSIAH. Loaned money for bounty, July, 1776. Collector of taxes, 1775; married Rebecca ——— before 1758; his widow died April 8, 1807; he died May 29, 1792; taxed in Medford, 1744-5 to 1792.

TUFTS, HUTCHINSON. Loaned money to pay bounty, July and Sept., 1776; son of Benjamin and Mary (Hutchinson); born Jan. 25, 1743; married Mary Grover, of Malden, Jan. 17, 1769; died Aug. 2, 1800; widow died, 1819.

TUFTS, JAMES. Loaned money to United States Government; loaned money for bounty, July and Sept., 1776. Son of James; taxed first in Medford, 1754, when part of Charlestown was annexed to Medford; married Tabitha Binford before that time; he died Nov. 5, 1786.

TUFTS, JOSEPH. Committee of correspondence, 1776; committee of safety, 1778; grand juror, 1775; loaned money for bounty, Sept., 1776. Born Feb. 21, 1731; son of Joseph and Lydia (Francis); died Dec. 6, 1778; taxed in Medford, 1761 to 1777; widow, Hannah, taxed 1778 to 1792.

TUFTS, JOSEPH, JR. Loaned money for bounty, July, 1776. Born Feb. 17, 1755; son of Joseph and Hannah; taxed in Medford, 1775 to 1794.

TUFTS, NATHAN. Loaned money for bounty, July and Sept., 1776. Son of Joseph and Lydia (Francis); born Oct. 5, 1741; married Elizabeth Tufts, Dec. 26, 1770; died June 12, 1784.

TUFTS, SIMON, ESQ. Loaned money for bounty for men enlisting to go to Canada, July, 1776; representative to General Court, 1772 to 1775; as trustee of estate of Isaac Royall he loaned money for bounty, 1776. Physician; he attended wounded soldiers after battle of Bunker Hill.

Son of Dr. Simon Tufts and Abigail Smith; born Jan. 16, 1727; graduated from Harvard, 1746; married, 1st, Lucy Dudley, daughter of Gov. Joseph Dudley; married, 2d, Elizabeth, daughter of Hon. Stephen Hall; died Dec. 31, 1786.

TUFTS, WILLIAM, JR. Loaned money for bounty, July, 1776. Born Sept. 4, 1727; son of John and Sarah ———; married Catherine Tufts (who married, 2d, Wyman, 3d, Richardson). Enlisted in expedition under Pepperell at age of 18; at siege of Louisburg, when the English were taking the Island Battery by storm, he was first to enter the works, climbed the flag staff, tore down the French colors, and put his red coat in its place to represent the English flag. He died April 27, 1782.

TURELL, EBENEZER, REV. Loaned money to town to pay bounty. Born Feb. 15, 1702; son of Samuel and Lydia (Stoddard); ordained and settled in Medford, 1724; died there, Dec. 8, 1778; married, 1st, Jane Colman, daughter of Rev. Benj. Colman, Aug. 11, 1726; 2d, Lucy Davenport, Oct. 23, 1735, and 3d, Jane Tyler, daughter of Wm. Pepperell of Kittery. This was her third marriage.

TURNER, WATTS. Loaned money for bounty, July and Sept., 1776. Son of John; baptized Oct. 17, 1742; married Hannah Tufts, daughter of Benjamin and Hannah (Turner), May 14, 1772; married, 2d, Ruhamah Brooks, Sept. 30, 1789; died Sept. 16, 1833.

TYSSICK, ———. Loaned money for bounty, Sept., 1776. Probably Joseph; see list of soldiers.

WADE, JOHN. Loaned money to pay bounty, July, 1776; also loaned money to the state for military purposes. Son of Nathaniel and Rebecca (Symonds), born 1742; married, 1st, Elizabeth Pool, daughter of Zachariah and Rebecca (Wade), Jan. 22, 1766; married, 2d, Rebecca, daughter of Edward Wade of Malden; occupation, leather dresser; his yard was at the foot of Simonds Hill, and his residence was on High street, opposite Bradlee road.

WARREN, ISAAC, DEACON. Committee of correspondence, 1773-1775; committee of safety, 1778 to 1781, inclusive. Son of Dea. John and Abigail ———; born Jan. 1, 1716, in Weston; died in Medford, Nov. 18, 1795 (gravestone); married, 1st, Ruth Hall, Nov. 19, 1741; 2d, Elizabeth Reeves, Oct. 3, 1754; 3d, Lydia, daughter of Hon. Ebenezer Burrell; she died Nov. 10, 1767 (gravestone); 4th, Sarah, who was admitted to church in Medford, Nov. 21, 1784 (parish records).

WILLARD, ———. Loaned money for bounty, Sept., 1776. [Ephraim Willard was taxed in Medford, 1776.]

WILLIAMS, GERSHOM. Loaned money to pay bounty, July and Sept., 1776; one of a committee to purchase beef; grand juror, 1781; occupation, victualler. Came with wife and children from "Parson Cook's Parish, Cambridge" (Arlington), April, 1772.

WINSHIP, ISAAC. Loaned money for bounty, July and Sept., 1776. Probably son of Isaac and Hannah; born April 7, 1749; married Sarah Fessenden, March 4, 1773; resided in Medford, and afterward in Lexington, where he was buried Dec. 1, 1834.

WINSHIP, SAMUEL. Loaned money for bounty, July and Sept., 1776. Probably son of Samuel and Hannah (Loring); born April 17, 1744; married Lucy, daughter of Stephen Hall, Tertius, 1768.

WYMAN, JAMES. Committee of correspondence, 1775; committee of prosecution, 1777; town treasurer, 1767 to 1778; representative to General Court, 1787; loaned money for bounty, Sept., 1776. Born Sept. 28, 1726, in Woburn; son of Joshua and Mary (Pollard); married Susanna Cutter, March 18, 1756; died Oct. 22, 1813.

ADDITIONAL

MILITARY RECORDS.

SOLDIERS OF THE REVOLUTION RESIDING IN MEDFORD BEFORE OR AFTER THE WAR.*

CARY, RICHARD, COL. Major in a Connecticut Regt.; brigade major, Aug., 1775, to June, 1776. See Carary, vol. 3, p. 86. Aide-de-camp to General Washington. Son of Richard and Elizabeth; born in Charlestown, Jan. 13, 1746-7; at Harvard, 1763; married, 1st., Anna Phillips, July 17, 1771; 2d, Anna Low. Came to Medford, 1777, and occupied Royall estate, Main street; during his residence there he was active in recruiting men for the army and in assisting soldiers' families; taxed in Medford, 1777 to 1783; his father was taxed in Medford, 1781 to 1786, and his brother, Samuel, 1777 to 1783. Col. Cary settled subsequently in Cooperstown, N. Y., and died after 1800.

FRANCIS, AARON. Residence, Beverly; in service as corporal, June 8, 1775; quartermaster in regiment of his brother, Col. Ebenezer Francis; served from Jan. 1, 1777, to April 16, 1782; vol. 6, p. 5. Born in Medford, Feb. 16, 1751; son of Ebenezer and Rachel (Tufts).

FRANCIS, EBENEZER, COL. Residence, Beverly; served as lieutenant, Lexington alarm; commissioned captain, 1775; organized regiment, Jan., 1777; killed at battle of Hubbardton, Vt., July 7, 1777; vol. 6, p. 9. Son of Ebenezer and Rachel (Tufts) of Medford; born Dec. 22, 1743.

FRANCIS, JOHN. Captain and adjutant; service, Jan. 1, 1777, to March 18, 1780; adjutant in regiment of his brother, Ebenezer; vol. 6, p. 9; born in Medford, Sept. 28, 1753; son of Ebenezer and Rachel (Tufts); residence, Beverly.

FRANCIS, LORING. Residence Lunenburg; service in R. I., 1779; vol. 6, p. 11. Born in Medford, June 7, 1762. See Richard.

*This list consists of a few names which I have found in the course of my researches; there has been no effort to make a complete record.

FRANCIS, RICHARD. Residence Lunenburg; service in R. I., 1779; vol. 6, p. 11. Richard and Loring were sons of Richard and Hannah (Winship); Richard, Sr., left Medford, 1768 or '69. Richard, the soldier, born in Medford, Dec. 16, 1760.

FRANCIS, THOMAS. Residence Beverly; sergeant, Lexington alarm; 1st Lieut., Feb. 20, 1777; served until Dec. 13, 1782; commissioned captain, 1780; vol. 6, p. 12. Brother of Col. Ebenezer Francis; born in Medford, July 15, 1748; resided in Medford, 1783 to 1790.

GATES, EDMUND TROWBRIDGE. Served in Continental Army, 1780; age 19; residence Framingham; vol. 6, p. 312. Born July 31, 1761; married Lucy Tufts of Malden, March 9, 1786; died in Medford, Oct. 1, 1822; taxed first in Medford, 1786.

POLLY, NATHANIEL. Enlisted at Framingham; served at Tiverton, R. I. Born in Medford, Feb. 8, 1761; son of Nathaniel and Mary; married, Oct. 18, 1781, Anna Maynard, of Framingham; he was then a resident of Sherborn. He learned trade of brickmaker, and in later life kept the half-way house between Boston and Providence, at South Walpole; died in Walpole, Oct. 30, 1830.

RICHARDSON, JAMES. Served 15 mos. as seaman on frigate *Alliance;* assisted in capture of British vessels, *Serapis* and *Countess of Scarborough,* 1779. Married Lucy, daughter of Paul Wyman, of Woburn (Revolutionary soldier), Dec. 26, 1781; died at Medford, Feb. 26, 1818; aged 56 (tombstone); widow drew pension. He is buried in Cross Street Cemetery, Medford.

STIMSON, EBENEZER. Served in Capt. John Brooks' company of Reading, Mass., April 19, 1775; afterward served 6 mos. in Continental Army. Son of Ebenezer and Eleanor; born in South Reading, 1749; married Esther Hartshorn, of Reading, 1780, and had 12 children; he died in Medford, 1829; buried in Cross Street Cemetery; resided in "Fountain House," Salem street, and owned a large tract of land in that vicinity; taxed in Medford, 1816 to 1829; heirs taxed, 1830; his daughter Eleanor married Nathaniel Jaquith of Medford.

SWAN, SAMUEL, MAJOR. Private, Dorchester Heights, 1776; 8 mos. service; no date (archives). Furnished provisions for army (board of war records; vols. 149 and 150); quartermaster-general in Northern army with rank major, under Maj. Gen. Benjamin Lincoln; also, quartermaster-general under Commissary Devens, at Ticonderoga, 1777; went there several times with provisions. He was also with Maj. Gen. Lincoln during Shay's Rebellion (papers in possession of

Swan family). Signer of petition for town meeting to act against importation of tea, 1773; March 20, 1777, town meeting (in Charlestown) adjourned to Maj. Swan's barn, at desire of persons lately living in Charlestown, who wished to be allowed to vote on town affairs; petition granted. May 26, 1777, chosen to procure evidence against tories; town clerk of Charlestown, 1779; treasurer, 1778 and 1780; one of recruiting committee, 1777, '80 (Charlestown records). Elected member of Ancient and Honorable Artillery, Jan., 1787; his father owned Bunker Hill Monument lot, and it was set off to him at his father's death; his family made its home in Medford when driven out of Charlestown; in 1791 he made Medford his permanent home. Born in Charlestown Jan. 17, 1750; son of Samuel and Joanna (Richardson); married Hannah Lamson, March 5, 1778; died Nov. 14, 1825. Father of Dr. Daniel Swan of Medford, Benjamin L. Swan of New York, and others.

TUFTS, FRANCIS. In 1775 enlisted from Lincoln Co. (Maine) for service at Tiverton, R. I.; 1776, in service at Dorchester Heights; 1775, 40 days' service on Penobscot river, dislodging tories who were stealing cattle (pension papers). Born in Medford July 21, 1744; son of Benjamin and Hannah (Johnson); married, 1st, in Medford, Nov. 26, 1767, Sarah Blount; 2d, Lydia (Blount) Blackstone, sister of first wife. He was one of three who purchased the present town of Farmington, Me., and sold it to settlers; emigrated to Maineville, O., at age of 87, making most of the trip on horseback; died in Maineville in 1833; aged 89; occupation, brickmaker; learned his trade in Medford.

ADDITIONS AND CORRECTIONS.
1930.

P. 34. CONERY, ISAAC. Served 3 mos. in New York, from July 10, 1780.* See Peter Conery.

P. 35. CUTTER, FRANCIS. 3 months' service in New York, from July 10, 1780.*

P. 36. DICKSON, ASA. Possibly this means Isaiah, brother of Isaac.

P. 37. EARL, WILLIAM. Married Martha Gill.

P. 37. FLOYD, ANDREW. (Additional service.) Served 3 mos. in New York, from July 10, 1780.*

P. 37. FLOYD, BENJAMIN. Date of death and age incorrect. Died July 17, 1817. Married, April 30, 1770, Rebecca Greenleaf.

P. 38. FRANCIS, BENJAMIN. In an unpublished letter from Rev. Convers Francis to William H. Whitmore it is stated that Benjamin Francis, grandfather (not uncle) of Lydia Maria Child was the soldier. He was born in Menotomy (now Arlington), 1734; married Lydia Convers; died in Medford, June 5, 1798, aged 64; occupation, weaver.

*See explanation under "Jeremiah Stewart."

P. 38. FRANCIS, JOSEPH. Married Elizabeth Usher, in Boston, May 15, 1764.

P. 39. GREEN, ISAAC. (Additional service.) Served 3 mos. in New York, from July 10, 1780.*

P. 42. KNIGHT, AMOS. Served at Tiverton, May, 1779, to July 1, 1779.*

P. 43. LeBOSQUET, JOHN. (Additional service.) Served 3 mos. in New York, from July 10, 1780.*

P. 44. OAKES, JOHN. Additional service and age, see "Mass. Soldiers and Sailors," v. 2, pp. 604, 599.

P. 45. PEIRCE, NATHANIEL. Served 3 mos. in New York, from July 10, 1780.*

P. 46. PORTER, JONATHAN. Born in Braintree, Mar. 12, 1745. Son of Dr. Jonathan and Hannah (Hayden).

P. 48. ROBBINS, NATHANIEL. Parents removed to Deer Isle, Maine, in spring of 1775.

P. 48. SIMONDS, JOSHUA. Son of Joshua and Rebecca Hamblett.

P. 49. STEWARD, AMASA. Son of Daniel and Mary (Ireland) of Lunenburg, Mass. Born, Dec. 18, 1768. Settled after war in that part of Camden, Maine, later Bloomfield, and now Skowhegan. Married there his cousin, Eunice Ireland. Removed to St. Albans, Maine, in 1829, and died there Sept. 10, 1845, aged 77 yrs., 3 mos. Pensioner.

P. 49. STEWART, JEREMIAH (Steward). Served 3 mos. in New York, from July 10, 1780. He was a relative of Amasa Steward. See above. The receipt and signature were found at City Hall, Medford, after this book was published, and are not included in list of Massachusetts Soldiers and Sailors of the Revolution, issued by the Commonwealth. They are now deposited at the State House, Boston.

P. 51. TUFTS, EBENEZER. Served 3 mos. in New York, 1780.*

P. 54. WADE, JAMES. Son of Samuel and Martha (Upham), who married first, Samuel Newhall.

P. 54. WATSON, JOHN. Served 3 mos. in New York, from July 10, 1780.*

P. 55. WILLSON, JOSEPH. (Additional service.) Served 3 mos. in New York, from July 10, 1780.*

P. 57. BROOKS, EBENEZER. Married Susanna, daughter of *Joseph* Thompson.

P. 61. POLLY, NATHANIEL. Son of Samuel and Elizabeth Hall. Married first, Sarah, second, Mary.

P. 61. SIMONDS, JOSHUA. Married Rebecca Hamblett.

P. 62. THOMPSON, JOSIAH. Born in Woburn, Dec. 2, 1724. Son of Ebenezer and Mary Winn. Married Rebecca Pratt.

P. 63. WARREN, ISAAC. Son of John and Abigail (Livermore). Married first, Ruth, daughter of Dea. Thomas Hall and Abigail Palfrey.

P. 63. TUFTS, WILLIAM, JR. Mistake caused by duplication of names. "The Hero of Louisburg" described died before 1775.

P. 66. GATES, EDMUND TROWBRIDGE. Married Elizabeth Tufts of Medford, 1786, *not* Lucy of Malden.

LEARNED, THOMAS. Served in 1775. Oct., 1777, served under Gen'l Gates. Was present at capture of Gen'l Burgoyne. In Rhode Island, 1778. Certificate of service destroyed by insane wife, 1805. Applied for pension, 1818. This record and affidavits of service of Gershom Teel, Robert Polly, and Edmund Trowbridge Gates were found in the Federal Building, Milk St., Boston, 1929, and transferred to the State Archives.

*See explanation under "Jeremiah Stewart."